The Politics of Compassion

The Politics of Compassion

Jack Nelson-Pallmeyer

ORBIS BOOKS

Maryknoll, New York 10545

© 1986 by Jack Nelson-Pallmeyer
Published by Orbis Books, Maryknoll, NY 10545
All rights reserved
Manufactured in the United States of America

Manuscript editor: William E. Jerman

Library of Congress Cataloging in Publication Data

Nelson-Pallmeyer, Jack
  The politics of compassion

  Bibliography: p.
  Includes index
  1. Sociology, Christian (Catholic)   2. Liberation
theology.   3. Hunger—Religious aspects—Catholic
Church.   4. Arms race—Religious aspects—Catholic
Church.   5. United States—Foreign relations—Central
America   6. Central America—Foreign relations—United
States   7. Catholic Church—Doctrines.   I. Title.
BX1753.N455   1986   261.8   85-25809
ISBN 0-88344-356-2 (pbk.)

But a Samaritan,
as he journeyed,
came to where he was;
and when he saw him,
he had compassion. . . .
Luke 10:33

Contents

Introduction

What has happened in the church would have been impossible twenty or thirty years ago. What has happened to the church in Latin America is extraordinary. I think about that when I go to the U.S. and see how the church is there. I think: you are so backward! And they never believe me. Because they think about the Third World, and assume we are underdeveloped. But as far as the church is concerned, my God, we are very developed! And then I have a great hope!

Sister Maria Hartman[1]

It was pitch black as I made my way down the hill in search of Padre Pedro. I groped my way toward a faint, distant light anchored to a small wooden structure that everyone calls the school, even though classes are usually held outside. I arrived in the middle of a Bible study and was immediately invited to participate. Three groups of Salvadoran refugees, now settled into an agricultural cooperative outside Managua, Nicaragua, were sitting with their Bibles open to the second chapter of Mark. Each group consisted of approximately ten to twelve persons. Two of the groups, including the one I had joined, were reading with the aid of flashlights. The participants were animated as they read, listened, and responded. Their elevated spirits were perhaps due to the fact that the ability to read was a new gift and itself a major accomplishment, or that Bible studies of this kind, which were routine in their new homeland, were regarded as acts of subversion in El Salvador. Their joy and satisfaction may also have been the result of the hope they felt as they consumed the words of Jesus like food that had been prepared especially for them.

The method of Bible study was simple, direct, and clear. Padre Pedro provided background to the book of Mark. He said that Mark is divided into two sections. The first, roughly the first nine chapters, is focused on Jesus' teaching, preaching, and especially his healing actions outside Jerusalem, in Galilee. The word of God and the actions of Jesus encounter resistance. Some individuals and groups like what Jesus does, but others oppose him. However, it is not until Jesus draws near to Jerusalem and eventually enters it, chronicled in the second half of Mark, that the full weight of opposition makes itself felt. It is in Jerusalem, the traditional center of economic, politi-

1

er, that opposition to Jesus builds and he is murdered.
ground filled in, the *campesinos* continued their Bible
p read Mark 2:1–12, in which Jesus heals a paralytic and
he second group gave special attention to verses 13–17, in
ticized by the scribes and Pharisees for eating with tax collectors
ne third group read verses 23–28, in which Jesus insists that the
ieant to serve rather than enslave. He therefore defends the actions
o.   ples who pluck grain on the Sabbath in order to satisfy their hunger.
Eac group read its particular verses three times as everyone listened intently
in the darkness. The discussion that followed centered on three basic questions:

1) What did Jesus do? (Not what did he *say* but what did he *do*?)

2) Whom did Jesus help and how?

3) Who was in opposition to what Jesus did, and why?

Each group took pains to be faithful to the text. *The actions of Jesus* included preaching, healing, forgiving sins, eating with tax collectors and sinners, and defending his disciples. *He helped* the paralytic, sinners, tax collectors, others who heard his message, the disciples, and perhaps—as one woman in the group speculated—others who were hungry and saw that for Jesus their hunger was more important than a rigid law. *Jesus was opposed by* the scribes and the Pharisees, who disliked his associating with sinners, his healing on the Sabbath, and his claim to forgive sins.

The responses to each of these questions were painstakingly recorded by a member of each group and later shared with the others. An old man in my group called to Padre Pedro, not for theological counsel, but to borrow his glasses so that with flashlight in hand he could see to write. He had recently learned how to write and each letter was like a new creation. I let a few tears flow as he finished his task with pride.

A second discussion centered on three additional questions:

1) Who is doing similar deeds today? (Not who is *talking like* Jesus but who is doing what Jesus did?)

2) Who is being helped by these Christlike actions, and how?

3) Who is in opposition to these actions today?

The life experiences of the *campesinos* flowed through the questions. The conflicts described in the second chapter of Mark, the healings and opposition to those healings, were easily related to their lives. The biblical story flowed through their own story, and the two became one. They recalled their hunger and poverty in El Salvador, the political and economic forces of oppression, and individuals and groups embodying love through social action. They viewed the assassination of Archbishop Romero as a continuation of the crucifixion of Jesus, and they remembered with a mixture of hope and sadness the many nuns, priests, and layworkers who stood with the poor until death—that is, until they got too close to Jerusalem or San Salvador—power centers. They remembered the grass-roots Christian communities that served the people but were the objects of unending repression. They talked about the death squads within the Salvadoran armed forces, the repeated promises and betrayals of land-reform programs, attacks on the popular organizations that sought to build political power, and the militarization of their country under the guise of U.S.-sponsored elections.

Their thoughts shifted to Nicaragua. Here their lives were different. They referred to the Nicaraguan government when they described the works of Jesus today. This government offered them refuge from the death and terror of El Salvador, provided them with land, technical assistance, low-interest loans, and markets for their produce. Their children were well-fed; signs of malnutrition had disappeared. They saw the divisions between Jesus and the scribes and Pharisees continuing in present-day Nicaragua. They contrasted the loving presence of Padre Pedro, who defended the rights and gains of the poor, with that of Cardinal Obando y Bravo of Managua, who consistently defended the interests of the rich. They contrasted the work of the Sandinistas, which had filled their lives with hope, with that of the U.S. government, which had destroyed the little they had had in El Salvador and continued to threaten their lives in Nicaragua.

In the presence of these *campesinos* I began to feel that my master of divinity degree earned at a seminary was about as valuable as a piece of scratch paper. Their experiences of poverty, repression, forced migration, resistance, endurance, suffering, and hope enabled them to understand the biblical message. These experiences also gave them the right and the credentials to teach me and others who, by virtue of our affluence, power, privilege, and isolation, are separated both from the biblical message and the people in whom that message is most clearly embodied today. We have eyes and ears but we are unable to see and hear, because of our isolation from God's messengers.

Two biblical passages came to mind as I sat in the midst of my *campesino* teachers:

Do you not yet perceive or understand? Are your hearts hardened? Having eyes do you not see, and having ears do you not hear? [Mark 8:17b–18a].

For consider your call, [brothers and sisters]; not many of you were wise according to worldly standards, not many were powerful, not many were of noble birth; but God chose what is foolish in the world to shame the wise, God chose what is weak in the world to shame the strong, God chose what is low and despised in the world, even things that are not, to bring to nothing things that are, so that no human being might boast in the presence of God [1 Cor. 1:26–29].

The *campesino* Bible study helped me to solidify an insight that had been evolving over more than a decade of work. For twelve years and continuing into the present I have been working with others to build bridges between those who suffer hunger and poverty due to political and economic injustice, and Christians living in North America, a center of world political and economic power. The insight stated simply is this: *Christians in North America, particularly those who are relatively affluent or comfortable, will understand the message of Jesus only if we let the poor be our teachers.* A closely related insight is that *we can seriously hope for a world with more justice and less hunger only if we understand history, economics, and theology from the vantage point of the poor.*

The task at hand for relatively affluent Christians living in North America entails nothing short of turning our world on its head. We are accustomed to reading the Bible and evaluating economic and political choices from the vantage point of privilege. We must discover how the poor can interpret the Bible for and with us. We must also learn to evaluate political and economic choices based on the impact they are likely to have on the poor and in consultation with the poor. It will not be easy for us to acknowledge the need for, let alone to help construct, bridges that will expedite sharing of the experiences, knowledge, and wisdom of *campesinos* and others. But this task is so important, so urgent, that it dare not be neglected.

The difficulty of opening our eyes and ears in new and creative ways to the biblical message and to the experiences of the poor was clearly demonstrated an hour after I left the refugee cooperative. After saying goodbye and thanks to the Salvadoran refugees, Padre Pedro and I went to La Casa de Estudios de Jaime Mayer (the James Mayer House of Studies) in Managua to meet with a group of Lutheran churchwomen from the United States. This house of studies, which my wife and I coordinate, is a project of the Center for Global Service and Education, headquartered in Minneapolis, Minnesota. The house of studies bears the name of James Mayer, a Lutheran missionary whose life was cut short by cancer but who had a profound impact on the Lutheran Church. His understanding of mission paralleled what I had experienced at the refugee cooperative—namely, that the purpose of mission is not to bring Jesus to the poor but rather to discover Jesus among the poor and oppressed, and enter into concrete struggles for liberation with them.

Padre Pedro explained to the North American churchwomen the method of Bible study used at the refugee cooperative. He went through the two sets of three critical questions, highlighted the controversial nature of Jesus' actions, and stressed the importance of discovering the *practice* of Jesus both as it was expressed in the original text and as it is expressed in the midst of society today. He then led the group in a study of part of the second chapter of Mark.

The contrast between what happened at the refugee cooperative and what happened at the Casa de Estudios could not have been more stark. The contrast began with the setting itself. The refugee cooperative was simple, spartan, and poorly illuminated. Our house is necessarily large (we house groups of up to twenty-two), comfortable, and well illuminated. There was none of the animation and excitement that had pervaded the refugee cooperative. The churchwomen, admittedly tired after a long day, showed little feeling for either the text or the methodology, and the evening ended with little discussion and only a few questions. Padre Pedro received few positive comments when the group filled out evaluation forms at the end of its stay in Nicaragua.

It is tempting to blame the failure of Padre Pedro's methodology—its failure to appeal to this relatively affluent group of churchwomen—on fatigue or on acceptable differences in ways of interpreting the meaning of faith. However, I believe it would be wrong to do so. There is a problem far deeper and more serious. The problem is that we are unable to hear the words of Jesus or to fully understand the significance of his actions because we are disconnected from the experiences of the poor and because we fail to acknowledge our dependence on them as teachers. The poor hold the key to our redemption and the first giant step toward this redemption is that we acknowledge that this is so.

This book was written for the nonpoor by a nonpoor person. If you are poor or non-Christian, it may still be of some value to you. However, it was written specifically for Christians who are reasonably well-off. Such a book, proposing to examine crucial biblical and social problems from the vantage point of the poor, might be more credible if authored by a poor person. (My wife and I live on an income whereby we are legally exempt from the payment of federal taxes. However, we understand that *involuntary poverty* is very different from *voluntary simplicity* chosen as an ideal to strive for. The difference lies precisely in the choosing. Latin American poverty is imposed on, not chosen by, those who endure it.)

The best that can be said is that I have tried to write from the perspective of the poor such as I have come to understand it. The book reflects not only the stories, experiences, and understanding of those who are poor and those who work directly with the poor in their struggle for liberation, but also changes in my life, feelings, actions, theology, and perspectives on politics and economics as a result of my interaction with the poor. The fact that my roots extend to very different worlds will, I hope, help the book bridge the gap between those worlds.

A brief sketch of the content and structure of what follows may be helpful. The book argues the need for Christians in North America to develop a politics of compassion that is rooted in biblical faith as a response to critical social problems such as hunger, the arms race, and U.S. policy in Central America. The fundamental assumption that serves as a foundation for this entire book is that *affluent Christians must let their faith and their politics, their economic and patriotic convictions, be challenged and transformed by the poor.* The problem is not simply that, if we ignore the causes of oppression and suffering, the poor will continue to suffer. The problem is also that, if we turn a deaf ear to the voices of the poor and cut ourselves off from their wisdom, we guarantee our own destruction.

I seek to develop a number of themes within the framework of the fundamental assumption stated just above:

First, we hear within the suffering of the poor the voice of God calling us to compassionate action. The fact that the suffering of the poor is often rooted in unjust social structures makes it imperative that a compassionate response be expressed in efforts to build political, economic and theological systems rooted in justice. Chapter 1 deals with these issues.

Secondly, a politics of compassion will grow from the roots of a liberated theology that learns from and expresses itself in concrete actions with the poor. The U.S.A., a world center of political, economic, and ideological power, must be transformed if the poor are to be liberated and if the world is to alter its disastrous course. This transformation is dependent on the conversion of Christians and churches in the United States. We must come to recognize elements in our traditional theology that discourage compassion. We must also look for elements that foster hope, commitment, and a longing for justice. These are the themes of chapter 2.

Thirdly, there are three vital issues that, if examined from the perspective of the poor, offer us concrete opportunities for conversion and politically embodied compassion. They are hunger, Central America, and the arms race, which are discussed in chapters 3, 4, and 5, respectively. These specific issues were chosen for the following reasons:

• The suffering of the poor, and God's voice heard within it, calling us to conversion and compassionate action, are clearly expressed in all three of these vital issues.

• The forces that cause and magnify these problems—the arrogance of power, the greed of economic interests, the idolatry of nationalism, the almost total blindness to the needs of the poor—are at work in all three issues.

• The three issues themselves are deeply interconnected. Hunger is a serious problem in Central America, and the political and economic injustices at the root of world hunger are deeply embedded there. At the same time, the global arms race, including its manifestation in Central America, exacts a heavy toll on the poor.

• Within the framework of each of these issues the poor have much to teach the nonpoor, as does the Bible when seen through their eyes and their experiences.

• The U.S.A., by virtue of its wealth and power, is of central importance in relation to these problems. Also within churches in the United States there is a growing concern about each of these issues and a growing commitment to compassion translated into political action.

• The issues of hunger, Central America, and the arms race have transformed and continue to transform my life and my faith, my work and my values. These issues have taken hold of my life during a decade of work with Clergy and Laity Concerned, the Hunger and Justice Project of the American Lutheran Church and the Lutheran Church in America, and most recently in my work with the Center for Global Service and Education. These issues, and the persons whose lives have become intertwined with mine through them, have become windows through which I have begun to learn about faith and politics from the poor.

Finally, if it is to be authentic, a politics of compassion must be rooted in hope that leads to concrete actions. Chapter 6 explores the relationship between hope and action, and offers specific suggestions for Christians living in North America on how to begin to confront and transform unjust social structures through compassionate action.

Chapter 1

A Call to Compassion

I listen to the agony of God—
I who am fed,
who never yet went hungry for a day.
I see the dead—
the children starved for lack of bread—
I see and try to pray.

I listen to the agony of God—
I who am warm,
who never yet lacked a sheltering home.
In dull alarm
the dispossessed of hut and farm
aimless and transient roam.

I listen to the agony of God—
I who am strong
with health and love and laughter in my soul.
I see a throng
of stunted children reared in wrong
and wish to make them whole.

I listen to the agony of God—
But know full well
That not until I share their bitter cry—
earth's pain and hell—
can God within my spirit dwell
to bring the Kingdom nigh.

"The Journey," Nancy Telfer[2]

7

ted when she showed the scars from some of the bullets that had
body as she stood waiting for a bus in San Salvador. She, like so
her innocent persons, was the target of a death squad, apparently with
ties to the government of El Salvador. Her crime was that she belonged to
women's organization that seeks to discover the whereabouts of *los desapare-
cidos*, the thousands of those who have disappeared, who are never seen again
or whose corpses turn up in shallow graves in various parts of the country.
Carmen's son, daughter, and brother all disappeared at the hands of death
squads.

I met Carmen in June 1984 in San Salvador. I was leading a group of U.S.
citizens on a tour of Central America sponsored by the Center for Global
Service and Education. The fact that Carmen lived is a miracle and she became
a miracle for others. At one point as she spoke to us this dignified woman
lowered the dress from her shoulder. She revealed a mass of scar tissue that had
once been a breast that had nurtured her now missing children. Government
security forces, not satisfied with machine-gunning her, had also cut off her
breast and left her for dead. But Carmen lived. She defied her murderers and
lived to tell her story, show her wounds, and call others to compassionate
action.

She spoke passionately as she called us to return to the U.S.A. to help break
the deadly alliance between the governments of the United States and El
Salvador. She believed that political justice in El Salvador and throughout
Central America would be possible only within the context of a profound
transformation of the political policies of the United States. She also believed
that this political transformation would be impossible without *a conversion of
Christians* within the U.S.A. that would enable them to become leavening
agents of justice.

Carmen's personal story, coupled with her political and religious challenges,
were painful messages for North Americans to hear. A woman traveling with
the program perceptively captured in biblical imagery part of the dynamic at
work in Carmen. Carmen was for her a Christlike figure willing to reveal
wounds, whereas so many others are like the doubting Thomas, needing to put
their fingers into Jesus' side—Carmen's bullet holes—in order to believe, to
feel the weight of the call of compassion, to commit themselves to action.

THE DEATH OF COMPASSION OR THE DEATH OF GOD?

A biblical name for the drying up of compassion is hardness of heart. The
biblical images of hardening one's heart or letting one's heart grow fat are used
to describe individuals and societies that have become blind to the pain and
suffering of others. Hardness of heart blocks grace and denies God's spirit,
which calls us to be compassionate in our individual conduct and to build
compassion into our corporate institutions and social systems.

The death of compassion is often confused with the death of God or with
God's abandonment of the world. In Taylor Caldwell's novel, *Captains and the*

Kings, the main character (Joseph) responds to his mother's untim
abandoning God:

> He put his head down near his mother's shoulder, near the youn⌣ ⌣⌣⌣⌣
> which had once nourished him, and her hand touched his hair with the
> gentle brushing of a wing, then fell. He held her other hand as if to
> withhold her from the darkness and the endless silence which he believed
> lay beyond life. He had seen many die, as young and innocent and as
> starving and brutalized as his mother, and helpless infants crying for food
> and old women gnawing their hands for hunger. He could not forgive
> God. He could no longer believe. He had only hate and despair to sustain
> him now, to give him courage.[3]

The momentum of agony that has been building up from Auschwitz,
Hiroshima, Vietnam, and a world food crisis has put God on trial. Is God
guilty of hardness of heart? Has God abandoned the world? The anger implicit
in such questions indicates that compassion is still alive. Outrage is an appropriate response to needless suffering and death. It is silence and resignation that
are condemnable.

Can there be authentic Christian faith that does not honestly wrestle with the
agony of the human situation? What kind of God reigns in the midst of
widespread hunger, poverty, and oppression? What does it mean to be Christian in a world on the brink of nuclear holocaust? The question of God's
hardness of heart or abandonment of the world can be a necessary step toward
our involvement in the world as responsible Christians. Hunger and the arms
race should put on trial both human compassion and our belief in an all-
powerful God. Christians who seriously consider the reality of hunger, economic exploitation, and injustice eventually meet a God who suffers.

The problem of God's apparent abandonment of history is really a problem
of the death of human compassion. The agony of the world, reflected in the
pain of millions of Carmens, causes God to suffer. The suffering of both the
world and God is alleviated when we become instruments of healing, hope, and
justice. God works through our compassionate action. Conversely, God suffers, and hunger and injustice thrive, when compassionate action slackens.
Jesus is crucified in the needless suffering of others. In other words, the death
of compassion results in the ongoing crucifixion of God.

THE COMPASSIONATE SAMARITAN

And behold, a lawyer stood up to put him to the test, saying, "Teacher,
what shall I do to inherit eternal life?" He said to him, "What is written in
the law? How do you read?" And he answered, "You shall love the Lord
your God with all your heart, and with all your soul, and with all your
strength, and with all your mind; and your neighbor as yourself." And he
said to him, "You have answered right; do this, and you will live."

But he, desiring to justify himself, said to Jesus, "And who is my neighbor?" Jesus replied, "A man was going down from Jerusalem to Jericho, and he fell among robbers, who stripped him and beat him, and departed, leaving him half dead. Now by chance a priest was going down that road; and when he saw him he passed by on the other side. So likewise a Levite, when he came to the place and saw him, passed by on the other side. But a Samaritan, as he journeyed, came to where he was; and when he saw him, he had compassion, and went to him and bound up his wounds, pouring oil and wine, then he set him on his own beast and brought him to an inn, and took care of him. And the next day he took out two denarii and gave them to the innkeeper, saying, 'Take care of him; and whatever more you spend, I will repay you when I come back.' Which of these three, do you think, proved neighbor to the man who fell among the robbers?" He said, "The one who showed mercy on him." And Jesus said to him, "Go and do likewise" [Luke 10:25-37].

I remember several sermons on this parable from my youth. They concluded with appeals that we stay out of trouble and be nice to others. I was a junior in high school when a severe football injury helped me to understand compassion a little better. I was in a body cast, told I might never walk again, and burdened by the prospect of an artificial hip. My world, which narrowly centered around athletics and a small Minnesota town, was collapsing. The compassion of my family and church members gave me hope and courage during that difficult time. I learned through the practical experience of their love that the essence of Christian faith is compassionate action. We are to love God and neighbor with all our heart, soul, strength, and mind (Luke 10:27).

The blessing of compassion that I experienced soon became for me a nightmare. I unconsciously began to view the world through the prism of compassion. The problem was that my world and my neighborhood then expanded beyond small towns and small problems to include Vietnam and world hunger. Napalmed children, villages destroyed in order to "save" them, antipersonnel weapons, deeply entrenched racism and inequality, widespread malnutrition and starvation did not look or feel good through the prism of compassion.

My expanded geography, in the form of emerging global awareness, together with the moral stretching that was encouraged by my experience of compassion from others, were extremely painful. I could not tolerate the injustice I saw through the prism of compassion, nor could I accept the indifference to injustice often reflected in my conduct and that of other Christians, including members of my own congregation. Persons who had opened their hearts to my need seemed to harden their hearts to the agony of the world at large. Compassion seemed bound by the familiar, the noncontroversial. It was nearly always associated with personal relationships and divorced from social problems such as economic exploitation, hunger, and hard-nosed militarism.

In the parable of the good Samaritan, a lawyer, "desiring to justify himself," asks Jesus, "And who is my neighbor?" Jesus responds with a description of a real-life situation. Many priests who served in the temple in Jerusalem lived in Jericho. Some of them were apparently returning home after completing their duties. Robberies were common along this road. A priest and a Levite came across a robbery victim—and passed by on the other side. But the Samaritan, "when he saw him, he had compassion, and went to him and bound up his wounds . . . and took care of him."

What is Jesus saying to us through this parable? First, *the parable of the good Samaritan is not about being good or bad; it is a story about compassion.* We often interpret the meaning of this parable from the perspective of *one* of the characters. "I am a good Samaritan because last week I helped Mr. Johnson chop wood." Or, "I'm just like the priest and Levite because yesterday I avoided Ms. Roberts who needed help with her garden." The problem with such an interpretation is that we individualize and personalize the meaning of the parable and therefore lose much of what it is saying. We either bask in the false glory of self-righteous behavior or we sink deeper into guilt, which reinforces our sense of our own worthlessness. The truth is that we are *all* of the characters in the story: lawyer, priest, Levite, Samaritan, and roadside victim. Each of us is capable of denying or giving birth to compassion.

If we affirm that each of us has the capacity to be either compassionate or hardhearted when confronted with difficult personal or social problems, then many new possibilities emerge. Grace can free us for involvement rather than pacify our guilt. Honesty about our complicity in problems such as hunger, torture, and the arms race may open us to the possibility of repentance and conversion concretely manifested through political action. Jesus' call to compassionate action can lead us to explore the personal and social forces in our lives that nurture or block compassion.

Secondly, *Jesus defines neighbor in a far broader sense than the lawyer expects.* The Jews could not imagine a good or compassionate Samaritan. Jews and Samaritans were enemies. The example of a compassionate Samaritan was repulsive to the lawyer. When Jesus asks, "Who proved neighbor to the man who fell among the robbers?," the lawyer could not bring himself to use the word "Samaritan." He responds instead, "the one who showed mercy on him." Jesus, by using a compassionate Samaritan in the story, is telling the lawyer that the breaking into history of God's kingdom involves a redefinition of neighbor.

One way of understanding the significance of Jesus' parable is to return to the story of the Salvadoran refugee cooperative in the Introduction. The U.S. propaganda campaign against the Sandinistas has been so strong that many a reader could be upset or confused when refugees refer to the Nicaraguan government as doing the work of Jesus in the world today. The assertion of the refugees was clearly validated by their experience and yet it runs counter to the prevailing image projected by those who shape U.S. public opinion. The idea of a good Samaritan was probably just as shocking to the lawyer in Jesus' parable.

Jesus broadens our understanding of neighbor in another way as well. The neighbor, and this is consistent with numerous Old and New Testament teachings, is whoever is in need—in the case of this parable, the robbery victim by the roadside.

Jesus' understanding of neighbor has profound implications for Christians seeking to live compassionately in the midst of widespread hunger and an escalating arms race. Our neighbors include persons who are racially, politically, culturally, religiously, or ideologically different from us. We meet neighbors who have a moral and economic claim on us wherever there is poverty, hunger, or oppression. We see God's compassion at work wherever individuals and groups combat poverty, hunger, and oppression with courage and integrity.

A third lesson from the parable is that *Jesus gives the term "neighbor" the force of a verb.* To "prove neighbor to" implies an active seeking on our part. The neighbor is one who seeks out others in need, "neighbors" them. Liberation theologian Gustavo Gutiérrez writes:

> The neighbor was the Samaritan who *approached* the wounded man and *made him his neighbor.* The neighbor . . . is not he whom I find in my path, but rather he in whose path I place myself, he whom I approach and actively seek.[4]

Being a neighbor implies action. We create a neighborly relationship between ourselves and others through compassionate action. Compassion or neighborliness is not simply a matter of sentiment or good intentions. It involves action that seeks to effectively alter the situation of those who are in need. The Samaritan "*had* compassion . . . *bound* his wounds . . . *set* him on his own beast . . . *brought* him to an inn . . . *took care* of him . . . and *gave*" money to the innkeeper.

There is desperate need to think of "neighboring" as a verb in a world of massive hunger threatened by nuclear holocaust. We become neighbors through compassionate action. The presence or absence of compassion between us and others passes sentence on the authenticity of our faith. "But if any one has the world's goods and sees [their] brother [or sister] in need, yet closes [their] heart against [them], how does God's love abide in [them]? Little children, let us not love in word or speech but in deed and in truth" (1 John 3:17–18).

Fourthly, *in the parable Jesus tells us that it is easier to be compassionate with those whom we know well or who are similar to us. Conversely, it is more difficult to be compassionate with those who are racially, economically, nationally, or otherwise different.* Jews disdained Samaritans; they were considered racially inferior and outside orthodox Judaism. Jews did not consider Samaritans their neighbors.

In a similar way, the members of my congregation found it relatively easy to show compassion to me when I struggled with the ramifications of a football injury. My family lived in their community and belonged to their church. I was a well-respected student and athlete. Napalmed children, on the other hand, were distant strangers. They were far away both physically and emotionally, considered by some to be racially inferior, or simply dismissed as communists.

I remember seeing on television an interview with a stoic U.S. general during the Vietnam war. The Vietnamese are different from us, the general insisted. They do not value human life and therefore they do not feel the anguish of death and destruction. But the camera then shifted to a village recently destroyed by a U.S. air strike. The tears, pain, rage, and passion on the faces of the villagers as they looked for loved ones belied the general's statement. Compassion requires identification with people who suffer. It means placing our fingers in Jesus' wounds, or feeling Carmen's scars from bullet holes and machete wounds. In this way the suffering becomes real as do the consequences of our silence.

"Crossing over to the other side of the road" can be a metaphor for distancing ourselves from the claims of others on our humanity. Suburban development is a means by which middle- and upper-class families physically separate themselves from the poor. Ideology is an effective tool of separation. The word "communist," for example, is often used to silence critics or distort debate about key issues, justify a monumental arms race that condemns millions of hungry persons to death, and cover up the carnage that often accompanies U.S. military support for repressive but anticommunist regimes. Racism and sexism are other common ways of keeping individuals and groups "out."

Against this backdrop of physical, ideological, and sociological separation from the poor, the parable of the compassionate Samaritan reminds us that compassion means identification with the needs and humanity of our neighbors. Samaritans were despised, ridiculed, abused, and oppressed. Perhaps daily experiences of oppression made the Samaritan in Jesus' story more likely to be in tune with the needs of someone who was beaten and left for dead on the road to Jericho. Jesus' call to compassionate action cuts through stereotypes of race, culture, and ideology, and affirms our common humanity, our oneness with God.

A fifth lesson from the parable is that *compassion is not something that can be legislated.* Levites and priests were religious professionals. They might be expected to be models of the faith. Not so. The Levite, priest, and Samaritan all lived under the injunctions of the Torah. Only the Samaritan acted compassionately. There is no indication that the Samaritan acted out of a sense of duty. The point is not that laws are bad or that Jesus was opposed to law. Jesus was a Jew who had great respect for Jewish law. He refers the lawyer to the law for an answer to the question about eternal life. However, Jesus opposed legalism, which violated the spirit and intent of the laws of God meant to encourage justice and compassion. Jesus understood that laws can be circumvented, ignored, or interpreted inflexibly. Compassion and the situation of the neighbor, on the other hand, daily implore believers to open their hearts to the pain of others and respond to their situation with compassionate action.

Laws are important but they cannot of themselves overcome hardness of heart or ensure justice. Most of the economic policies that result in widespread hunger are legal. Despair, indifference, callousness, and selfishness can be legal. Fair and equitable legal systems are a necessary component of justice but they are not a substitute for compassion. Jeremiah envisioned a time when God would establish a new covenant that would bring law and compassion together: "I will put my law within them, and I will write it upon their hearts; and I will be their God and they will be my people" (Jer. 31:33). Jesus ushers in the new covenant whose hallmark is compassion.

Sixthly, *compassion is risky.* In judgmental moments I condemn the indifference to human suffering reflected in the behavior of the priest and Levite in the parable. How could they be so callous as to pass by on the other side? Some time ago in Addis Ababa, Ethiopia, I understood their situation more clearly. In Addis Ababa in 1972 it was nearly impossible to avoid confronting beggars. Some were grossly deformed. At first their situation moved me deeply. However, I grew weary of their presence as time went on. I literally crossed to the other side of the road to avoid them. Sometimes a five-minute walk took me twenty minutes because of the zigzag path I followed!

Compassion demands emotional and physical risk. We need to rip open our consciences and explore our complicity in the suffering of others. Those of us who are adequately fed should acknowledge our fear of being victims. We should also be honest and say that we are glad that we are not hungry but that we often express our gratitude in ways that are fearful and self-centered rather than compassionate.

One reason why we are afraid to take risks for others is our enslavement to a sense of powerlessness and guilt. We assume the inadequacy of our response to complicated issues such as hunger, injustice in Central America, and the arms race, and thereby condemn ourselves and others to self-fulfilling prophecies of gloom. Ironically, to be compassionate we must recognize the inadequacy of a faith that leads to despair and inaction even as we acknowledge our dependency on faith as the wellspring from which hopeful and compassionate lives and actions flow. Many Christians and their churches are deeply cynical about solving problems such as hunger and the arms race. But cynicism is a denial of the gospel that calls us to be a people of hope and compassion.

Compassion may involve risking bodily harm as well as emotional distress. One example familiar to many is the growing number of reports about persons who stand silently by as others are beaten, robbed, or killed. Other stories describe how "good Samaritans" who dare to intervene to help others are themselves beaten, robbed, or killed.

The murder of Archbishop Oscar Romero in El Salvador is a less familiar example of the risk involved in compassionate living. Oscar Romero lived and died befriending the vast majority of the people of El Salvador, victims of economic injustice, victims of death squads with close ties to the government, and victims of U.S. foreign policies that reinforce terror. Archbishop Romero was assassinated while celebrating Mass shortly after he had sent a letter to

President Carter urging him to stop the flow of weapons to El Salvador. In his daily work with his people and priests Romero saw how U.S. weapons accounted for the deaths of innocent Salvadorans.

Romero sealed his fate when he urged Salvadoran soldiers to stop killing their brothers and sisters, and to obey God rather than their military superiors when they were given an order contrary to the law of God:

> I want to make a special appeal to soldiers, national guardsmen, and policemen: Brothers, each one of you is one of us. We are the same people. The *campesinos* you kill are your own brothers and sisters.
>
> When you hear the words of a man telling you to kill, remember instead the words of God, "Thou shalt not kill." No soldier is obliged to obey an order contrary to the law of God. . . .
>
> In the name of God, in the name of our tormented people who have suffered so much and whose laments cry out to heaven, I beseech you, I beg you, I order you in the name of God, *stop the repression!*[5]

Oscar Romero knew that economic and governmental injustice blocked human compassion. He also understood that the price of standing compassionately with the poor in opposition to injustice would be persecution of the church and probably his own death. Compassionate resistance is costly but so also is silence. Silence in the face of injustice means the death of innocent bystanders, betrayal of the gospel, and the undoing of human compassion. Romero said:

> It is the poor who force us to understand what is really taking place. . . . The persecution of the church is a result of defending the poor. Our persecution is nothing more nor less than sharing in the destiny of the poor.[6]

In the compassionate Samaritan story Jesus tells us something about religious hypocrisy. He also tells us something about taking risks. The victim in the parable, beaten and left by the roadside, is said to be half dead. According to Jewish law had he died while the priest, Levite, or Samaritan were helping him, they would have been defiled for touching a corpse (Lev. 19). Compassionate action involved risking seven days of seclusion. If the priest in Jesus' story is a high priest, then it is all the easier to understand why he might cross to the other side: the penalty for a high priest who touched a corpse was *disbarment from the priesthood for life.*[7] Compassion is risky.

PERSONAL COMPASSION AND THE NEED FOR SOCIAL CHANGE

Imagine that the compassionate Samaritan in Jesus' story travels the same road each day for six months. Every day he confronts another robbery victim who is beaten and left for dead. What do you think his response would be? I simplify things here by limiting the Samaritan's response to three likely choices. The Samaritan might:

• demonstrate incredible patience and continue to meet the needs of each victim;

• become discouraged and cross to the other side of the road;

• move beyond either of the first two responses and make a commitment to discover *why* so many are being victimized and what must be done to correct the situation.

If we banish the Carmens from our neighborhood and lose contact with others who deeply touch our humanity, then compassion dies. However, compassionate action is often ineffective or short-lived unless it addresses the sources and systems of injustice. I remember the story of a pastor who helped organize a drive to bring surplus food from farmers in rural Minnesota to urban areas with high unemployment and serious poverty. He felt satisfied and proud of himself and others after dropping off a final truckload of food to distribution centers. He was less pleased when he turned on the radio to hear that a few hours earlier the U.S. Congress had enacted massive cuts in federal feeding programs. These budget cuts were a hundred thousand times greater than the value of the food distributed by his voluntary effort. The budget cuts did not mean that the compassion of thousands of persons and months of time and energy had been wasted. They did demonstrate how compassion must seek institutional outlets as well as be embodied in individual conduct.

Massive hunger and the threat of nuclear holocaust call Christians to compassionate actions that involve personal and social change. It is a call that must penetrate the hearts of Christians living in the United States. Miguel D'Escoto, Catholic priest and foreign minister of Nicaragua, states the challenge:

> I would like to say a word to people who are directly informing religious people. They have a terrific obligation to wake up religious people to their responsibilities because . . . that is the greatest fault that I see in American society. The leavening agent has lost its potency. I think the problem . . . [in the United States] is not technological; it's a problem of the heart, atrophying, not growing with the same rhythm that other things grow. It's a problem of the heart.[8]

Chapter 2

The Liberation of Theology

Vos sos el Dios de los pobres,
El Dios humano y sencillo;
El Dios que suda en la calle,
El Dios de rostro curtido.
Por eso es que te hablo yo
Así como habla mi pueblo;
Porque sos el Dios obrero,
El Cristo trabajador.

You are the God of the poor,
The simple human God;
The God who sweats in the street,
The God with a weathered face.
That is why I speak to you,
As my people speak;
Because you are the laborer God,
The worker Christ.

Song from the Nicaraguan *Campesino* Mass,
by Carlos Mejía Godoy

It is both sad and ironic that the biblical message, which calls us to be a people of hope, compassion, justice, and peace, has been so distorted as to become a principal obstacle to compassion and a major contributor to world hunger, economic injustice, and the arms race. The problems of hunger and the threat of nuclear holocaust call us to compassionate action and demand a rethinking of the meaning of Christian faith. This is the purpose of the present chapter, which seeks to find a way to liberate theology from its complicity with injustice and reestablish it as a potent force for personal and social compassion and for change. The search for theological insight continues in chapter 5, where the biblical message is explored in light of the arms race.

17

A reassessment of theology is not without its pitfalls. I am a believer, a student of theology, and a person whose actions are shaped by my understanding of the Christian faith. However, human propensity to misuse scripture makes me reluctant to let the Bible speak to our historical situation of hunger. The Bible has been used to justify slavery and the subjugation of women. Today, belief sometimes spills over into fanaticism fueling moral passions and religious wars. The Central Intelligence Agency (CIA) and other powerful groups resort to manipulation of religion as a means to pursue U.S. foreign policy goals. Issues such as prayer in public schools shed darkness rather than light on problems of national priorities relative to religious values. The misappropriation of religion evident in these and many other examples speaks to the need for caution when looking to the Bible for guidance in the complex world.

The problem of misusing scripture is compounded by the question of who decides when scripture is being used appropriately or inappropriately. The Bible always speaks through someone or some group. Its message is funneled through the experiences of those who wrote or translated the original material and by those who present or listen to it today. The Bible is not a single book but a variety of books and stories written over a period of hundreds of years by writers facing different circumstances including slavery, landlessness, exile, religious persecution, and foreign domination. It should not be surprising that the God revealed to a people whose faith grew out of varied experiences is a complex and seemingly inconsistent God—a God who permits slavery and takes the initiative in liberation from slavery, judges harshly, and dies a redemptive death on a cross. The complexity and diversity of scripture is fertile ground for both insights and distortions.

Christians who wish to relate their faith to complex realities such as hunger or economics need to remember that the Bible is not an economic or political treatise. It does not provide a blueprint by which we can construct a "Christian economy" or discern a "Christian course of action" for all possible life-situations. Faith is a journey, more analogous to the diversity of poetry than to the rigidity of a true-or-false quiz.

The absence of a political blueprint does not mean that Christian faith is unrelated to economic problems or that we are left alone to sail uncharted waters when it comes to determining compassionate responses to social problems such as hunger. The Bible can speak with power and authority to problems of hunger and economic injustice in the twentieth century. However, it cannot tell us the exact nature of those problems nor can it dictate precise solutions. We must avoid two pitfalls: the temptation to dismiss the biblical message as hopelessly relative and subjective; and the temptation to carve relevant insights into stone as if they were absolute truths. If we avoid these pitfalls, then the Bible can help guide our understanding and action vis-à-vis social problems.

A COLONIAL THEOLOGY

For several years at a Lutheran seminary in Minnesota, I taught a course on hunger and the arms race. Some of my students insisted that Christians differ over means, not ends. All Christians, they argued, are interested in human well-being, worshiping God, and salvation. If they differ, it is over the means to living out these concerns. But this is only partly true. For example, there is a profound difference between the goal of "saving souls" and that of ministering to the spiritual, physical, and emotional needs of individuals and communities. It was thought permissible during the colonial period to enslave, economically exploit, torture, and even kill persons while you were "saving" them. Physical well-being was unrelated to the religious task of "converting condemned souls" to Christ.

The differences among Christians over the goals and means of ministry remain stark in the hungry world of today. Central and Latin America are experiencing a dramatic influx of fundamentalist groups and sects whose theology and politics align them with right-wing military governments. Most are funded by conservative churches in the United States.[9] On the other hand, the passion for social change in Central and South America can be understood only in the perspective of Christians seeking to be faithful to the liberating message of Christ.

The emergence of a theology of liberation and of small, grass-roots communities of Christians (base Christian communities) studying the word of God in light of their experience of oppression and their longings for justice are at the root of movements for social change. Not surprisingly, conservative groups aligned with economic injustice in Latin America have attacked liberation theology and linked it to communist subversion. The Santa Fe Report, prepared by the Council for Inter-American Security, has served as an ideological foundation for the Reagan administration policies in Latin America. It offers this critique of liberation theology:

> U.S. foreign policy must begin to counter . . . liberation theology as it is utilized in Latin America by the "liberation theology" clergy. . . . Unfortunately, Marxist-Leninist forces have utilized the church as a political weapon against private property and productive capitalism by infiltrating the religious community with ideas that are less Christian than communist.[10]

A high-ranking official at the U.S. embassy in Managua told me that the religious problem in Nicaragua can be seen in terms of a contest between those who wish to save souls (an option he clearly endorsed) and those who believe that Christians should also concern themselves with bettering human lives on earth.

Theology informs the conduct of Christians in ways that encourage either liberation or subjugation, caring or indifference, compassionate action or disengagement. It is ironic that numerous biblical passages condemn hunger and see it as a sign of spiritual brokenness, whereas the theology of many Christians ignores or reinforces the causes of world hunger. Christians and their churches have often, knowingly or unknowingly, ratified or tolerated unjust economic relationships that lead to hunger and starvation.

The tragic marriage of distorted theology and economic oppression is characteristic of the colonial period. Colonialism was marked by economic injustice, including:

- the pillaging of gold, silver, and other minerals;
- the enslavement of peoples who were forced through economic or military means to work the mines or lands of others;
- the theft of land, which often included the elimination of communal holdings and the formation of large holdings owned by elites, including the church;
- a dramatic shift in land use away from local food production to export commodities demanded by colonizing powers;
- the development of infrastructures designed to move goods out of a country rather than to distribute goods and services internally.

Economic injustice was reinforced by the dominant theology of the period. Missionaries "saved souls" while colonizers plundered indigenous people, land, and gold. Indigenous cultures were destroyed along with indigenous economies. Elements of colonial theology included:

- the strict separation of body and soul, heaven and earth;
- the acceptance of poverty as God's will and of wealth as a sign of God's approval;
- obedience to church and state authority despite whatever misery they cause;
- a stress on individualism above community need in matters of spiritual salvation and material economics;
- the pacifying promise of a heavenly reward.

Hunger is a direct result of the distorted theology and economy of the colonial period. These distortions live on today in the international economy and in Western theology. The reality of mass hunger, which forces me to question the values, assumptions, and efficacy of the international economy (chap. 3), also challenges the dominant theology of Western churches.

GOD'S TRANSFORMING LOVE AND THE REALITY OF HUMAN SIN

The underlying theme of the Bible is God's transforming love confronting the reality of human sin. Sin is embodied in individual conduct, social systems, self-serving theologies, warped values, and unjust economic structures. God's love is expressed through prodding and judgment, healing and nurturing, compassion and forgiveness. The different expressions of God's love are united by a single purpose: to confront and transform sinful situations. God's love infuses light where there is darkness, hope where there is despair, compassion where there is pain. This is what the Bible calls salvation. It is surprising that persons who are bound by sin are seen by God as both recipients and agents of God's transforming love. We are freed by God's love to be a people of hope, liberation, and healing. Jesus announces that "today salvation has come to this house" (Luke 19:9) after the tax collector, Zacchaeus, promises to make restitution to anyone he has defrauded. He becomes God's servant, rather than seeking the satisfaction of selfish desires or currying favor with Rome.

The biblical writers view the imposition of hunger and economic injustice as sin that blocks compassion and oppresses victims and perpetrators alike. A liberating theology expresses the transforming power of God's love, which can free us, at least partially, from our bondage to sin. Some principles of a liberating theology include the following:

• Faith is a journey with God at the center of personal and community life. It is not primarily a statement of belief.

• God is an advocate for the poor. The liberation of rich and poor is part of the same historical process.

• Our relationship to the poor and their well-being is a yardstick by which we can measure the integrity of our faith.

• Salvation, redemption, and baptism have historical consequences; they reflect how deeply God cares about history.

• The legitimacy of economic priorities and systems can be judged in terms of socio-economic equity and the well-being of the poor.

Faith—A Journey

Faith is not a once-in-a-lifetime or often-repeated proclamation of belief. It is a commitment by individuals and communities to embark on or continue a journey with God as the center of life. The life and teachings of Jesus implore us to *come follow*. Jesus was impatient with verbal statements of commitment that were not followed by action. "Not every one who says to me, 'Lord, Lord,' shall enter the kingdom of heaven but [those] who [do] the will of God" (Matt. 7:21). In the Gospel of Mark he says: "Why do you call me 'Lord, Lord,' and not do what I tell you?" (6:46).

This is not to say that belief or trust are unimportant. The degree to which we believe in or trust someone or some group determines how open, vulnerable, or committed we will be to them. In a similar way, the belief or trust we have in God will determine our willingness or unwillingness to embark on an open-ended journey with God at the center of our lives. Faith is easy for some Christians because it has been reduced (wrongly) to verbal statements and predictable rituals such as Sunday morning worship. Faith is difficult for others because it means surrendering certitude in favor of trusting that God will guide us on a journey that involves living with questions rather than clinging to the security of pat answers.

The Bible narrates many stories about persons of faith embarking upon journeys. "By faith Abraham obeyed when he was called to go out to a place which he was to receive as an inheritance, *and he went out, not knowing where he was to go*" (Heb. 11:8; italics added). Moses went out to tend a flock of sheep—and met God (Exod. 3:ff.). The oppression and suffering of the Israelites at the hands of the Egyptians angered God. Moses, commissioned by God, was led by faith to confront the pharaoh, organize the enslaved Hebrews, and enter the wilderness in search of a homeland. God also seemed to be on a journey. Moses wanted to describe God to the Israelites and so he asked God for a self-description. "God said to Moses, 'I AM WHO I AM. . . . Say this to the people of Israel, I AM has sent me to you' " (Exod. 3:14). The phrase "I am who I am" (Yahweh) is the personal name of the God of Israel and is sometimes translated "I will be what I will be." [11]

The faith journeys of the prophets included conflicts with kings and religious leaders, exile, imprisonment, and sometimes death (Jer. 26:7-11; 37:15; Amos 7:10-14). Mary and Joseph fled with their son to avoid the wrath of Herod (Matt. 2:13). Simon and Andrew left aside their means of support in order to follow Jesus (Mark 1:16-18). Zacchaeus met Jesus and ended up with only a fraction of the wealth that had been his prior to the encounter (Luke 19:5-9). Another rich man turned away sad because the cost of a journey of discipleship was too high (Luke 18:18ff.). Paul was beaten, ridiculed, and imprisoned on numerous travels in service to God and the church (2 Cor. 11:23-28).

There was also the faith journey of Jesus. Jesus was not a robot-god programed by a divine power to carry out a predetermined mission. He entered the wilderness, prayed, fasted, and repeatedly searched for clues to the mystery of God's will for his life. Jesus' faith put him in conflict with religious and political authorities and in contact with the poor and the powerless. Ultimately, his faith journey led to a cross, a prospect he told his disciples they would likely have to face (Luke 9:23-25).

We are ready to accept change in our lives when we embrace faith as a journey. God's transforming love then has room to maneuver. Understanding that God loves me enough to disrupt my life was a major turning point in my faith. God is trying to get our attention in a world of massive hunger and widespread silence. Our lifestyles, jobs, economy, ideology, faith, and theology need disrupting if we are to become a people of hope and compassion. I sometimes experience God's love as great joy. However, disrupting encounters with God feel like a baseball bat has been thrust into my stomach. I come up gasping for air and with a lasting pain in my gut.

Moses, the prophets, and Jesus were led by faith into a wilderness. The image of a wilderness—dark, dangerous, and foreboding—captures how it sometimes feels to have our lives disrupted by a loving God.

"I believe" are words that affirm our trust in God and our willingness to travel a road filled with changes. The voices of the hungry cry out to us as God's call to compassionate action. Individuals, communities, churches, and societies are asked to undertake a journey that will lead to a closer and more just relationship with the poor. This journey holds the key to the liberation of rich and poor, hungry and nonhungry, oppressed and oppressors.

God—Advocate for the Poor

The theme of God's advocacy of the poor is central to the biblical message. The exodus story is an account of God's liberating activity to free an oppressed people. The poor claim with confidence that "the Lord is on my side to help me" (Ps. 118:7). The biblical message is good news to the poor because the Lord loves justice (Isa. 61:8); is a stronghold to the poor and needy (Isa. 25:4; Ps. 9:9); hears the desire of the meek, strengthens their hearts, and does justice to the orphan and the oppressed (Ps. 10:17–18); hears the groans of prisoners and sets free those who are condemned to die (Ps. 102:20); hears the cry of the hungry (Ps. 107:4–6); raises the poor from the dust and lifts the needy from the ash heap (Ps. 113:7); maintains the cause of the afflicted and executes justice for the needy (Ps. 140:12). Those who oppress the poor insult their Maker (Prov. 14:31), and the Lord pleads the cause of the poor and despoils those who despoil them (Prov. 22:23).

That God takes sides is explicit in Psalm 12:5:

> "Because the poor are despoiled,
> because the needy groan,
> I will arise," says the Lord;
> "I will place [them] in the safety
> for which [they] long."

The New Testament affirms God's special relationship to the poor. Jesus and his disciples were poor and lived among the poor. God's favor toward the poor is explicit in the Beatitudes (Luke 6:17, 20–23; Matt. 5:3ff.) and in the Magnificat (Luke 1:53). Jesus announces the goals of his ministry in his first sermon in Luke: "to preach good news to the poor," "set at liberty those who are oppressed," and "proclaim the acceptable year of the Lord" (4:18–19).

The assertion that God is an advocate for the poor invites hostility from the wealthy. The biblical message often confronts us at the point of greatest resistance, our ultimate allegiances, our idols. Jesus says we cannot worship God and money (Matt. 6:24) and yet we are often slaves to the lifestyles, power, and ideology that flow from wealth. The assertion that God is an advocate *for* the poor is most upsetting because of the implication that God is therefore *against* the rich. Others, bound by an ideology of grace, resist any discussion of God in relation to wealth and poverty. In their view any such discussion inevitably leads to the problem of works/righteousness. We are saved by grace, not works, their argument runs, and therefore questions of wealth and poverty are of little importance.

The problem of God's relationship to rich and poor is compounded by the inconsistency within scriptures. There are three important biblical themes dealing with these issues. The first two are contradictory and the third offers the possibility of transformation.

First, there are the *woe sayings*. These should make all of us who are not poor uneasy. A woe saying is the announcement of a funeral. "Woe to you" means "death to you":

> Woe to those who lie upon beds of ivory,
>   and stretch themselves upon their couches,
>   and eat lambs from the flock,
>   and calves from the midst of the stall [Amos 6:4].

> Woe to those who join house to house
> who add field to field,
> until there is no more room,
> and you are made to dwell alone
> in the midst of the land [Isa. 5:8].

But woe to you that are rich, for you have received your consolation. Woe to you that are full now, for you shall hunger [Luke 6:24–25].

Passages that link wealth to death are generally ignored by the rich. They choose instead to focus on a second aspect of the biblical message: *wealth as a sign of God's blessing.* Several verses from Proverbs illustrate this perspective:

> I love those who love me,
> and those who seek me diligently find me.
> Riches and honor are with me,
> enduring wealth and prosperity.
> My fruit is better than gold, even fine gold,
> and my yield than choice silver.
> I walk in the way of righteousness,
> in the paths of justice,
> endowing with wealth those who love me,
> and filling their treasuries [8:17–21].

> Misfortune pursues sinners,
> but prosperity rewards the righteous [13:21].

There are enough examples like these in scripture to allow us to proof text our way into self-serving ideologies. Belief that wealth is a sign of blessing is a colonial inheritance that is presently a part of the national mythology of the United States. President Lyndon Johnson boasted to the convention of Junior Chamber of Commerce Executives in 1967:

Although we have only about 6% of the population of the world we have half its wealth. Bear in mind that the other 94% of the population would like to trade with us. Maybe a better way of saying it would be that they would like to exchange places with us. I would like to see them enjoy the blessings that we enjoy. But don't you help them exchange places with us—because I don't want to be where they are. Instead, I believe that we are generous enough—I believe that we are compassionate enough—and I believe that we are grateful enough that we would like to see them enjoy the blessings that are ours.[12]

A national mythology of wealth as a verification of divine blessing runs counter to the overall thrust of scripture, which considers wealth the result of economic exploitation of the poor and an obstacle to both compassion and spiritual health. The rich are like a "partridge that gathers a brood she did not hatch" (Jer. 17:11); they store up violence and robbery in their strongholds (Amos 3:10; Micah 6:11-12); they become wealthy through wickedness (Jer. 5:27-28).

The third perspective of the biblical message is that *wealth in the midst of hunger, poverty, and economic injustice is a sign of spiritual brokenness.* Where there is wealth *and* poverty there is an absence of compassion and a need for transformation and healing that involves both the rich and the poor. God's advocacy of the poor is necessary for the liberation of both rich and poor. The rich are spiritually bankrupt because their unjust wealth denies the poor the basic goods they need for spiritual health and physical sustenance.

God is an advocate for the poor in order to be an advocate for the rich who must be freed from the wealth that shackles them and blocks their participation in the kingdom (Luke 18:24-25). It is in this sense that the redemption of the rich is dependent on the liberating actions of the poor. A rich man in the Gospel of Mark asks Jesus what he must do to inherit eternal life. Jesus looks at him, *loves* him, and then tells him to sell what he has, give it to the poor, and come follow him (10:21). Love is the motivating force behind advocacy for the poor.

The argument raised earlier that the dangers of the works/righteousness problematic preclude discussion of issues related to wealth and poverty totally misses the point. We have no right and little scriptural basis to speculate about wealth and poverty in relation to final judgments. The biblical message is conflicting and confusing on this point. In Matthew 25 those who ignore the needs of the hungry ignore Jesus and are told: "Depart from me, you cursed, into the eternal fire prepared for the devil and his angels" (v.41). The rich man in the Gospel of Luke ignores the suffering Lazarus, dies, and is tormented in Hades (16:22-23). On the other hand we are told to love our enemies because God makes the sun rise on the evil and on the good, and sends rain on the just and the unjust (Matt. 5:45). Paul's theology of grace can be summarized in two verses from Romans: "For there is no distinction; since all have sinned and fall short of the glory of God, they are justified by . . . grace as a gift, through the redemption which is in Christ Jesus" (3:22-23).

Those who speak with certainty about final judgments are walking on thin ice. This is God's turf, not ours. We can and must say that *unjust relationships between rich and poor and the distorted economies that feed them have profound and destructive material and spiritual consequences.* Their implications for the afterlife may be hazy but their historical consequences are clear. They block human compassion and foment a deep material and spiritual crisis. Persons without adequate food are materially impoverished. Persons who are well-fed *and* indifferent to or exploitive of others are spiritually impoverished. The biblical teachings on God's advocacy for the poor and on the dangers of wealth point the way to the liberation of both rich and poor.

The Integrity of Our Faith

God's transforming love seeks to overcome sin and free us to be instruments of hope, healing, and compassion. In this context, hunger and our complicity in structures that perpetuate it are scandalous. God's healing love seeks to move us from complicity to compassion. Our faith is central to this task, but how? Part of the answer is to embrace faith as a journey. Faith in God is often firm at the deepest part of our being, but discerning where God wishes to lead us requires openness and risk taking. How do we know if we are on the right track? How can we avoid the pitfalls of sects and individuals whose faith journeys appear to be self-serving or headed toward dead ends?

The Bible gives us a relatively simple guideline by which we can assess, within rough bounds, the integrity of our faith journey: *our relationship to the poor.* This guideline can also help us reflect critically on the life of our faith community and on the theology of our churches. The colonial theology mentioned earlier, for example, is intrinsically flawed, as can be seen by its impact on the poor.

Theology that ignores, tolerates, or exploits poverty and the poor is unbiblical, destructive, and self-serving. In contrast, Amos, for example, is concerned about the *religious* as well as the economic implications of the worsening social inequality that results from exploitation of the poor. A passage from my earlier book, *Hunger for Justice*, describes the economic reality:

> While foreign trade and the changing social fabric meant wealth and power for merchants and the emerging urban class, they undermined the well-being of growing numbers of people. Amos consistently condemns the wealth of the rich, which has been gained by exploiting the poor (Amos 2:6–7; 3:10; 4:1; 5:11–12), and he is particularly irate that the affluent social classes in Israel live in luxury far removed from the suffering on which that luxury is based (Amos 6:1–7). Indeed, archeological excavations near the site of Amos's prophecy have uncovered distinct sections of the city; one containing large, expensive houses of luxury, the other, small, huddled structures.
>
> Farmers were particularly victimized during this period. Small landowners were forced off their land and their property passed into the hands of urban elites. Displaced farmers constituted a new economic class of landless serfs who worked the vineyards and farms for their new overlords. Urban elites transformed independent farmers into tenants and they built large estates on the backs of the poor. Often a tenant would turn over a major portion of the grain produced as payment for use of the land.[13]

Persons of faith respond to the deteriorating situation of the poor in Israel with silence. The temples are filled, religious rituals are performed, and sacrifices take place *as if the exploitation of the poor did not matter.* God judges the integrity of the religious life of the people through the words of Amos:

> I hate, I despise your feasts,
>   and I take no delight in your solemn assemblies.
> Even though you offer me your burnt
>   offerings and cereal offerings,
>   I will not accept them,
> and the peace offerings of your fatted beasts
>   I will not look upon.
> Take away from me the noise of your songs:
>   to the melody of your harps I will not listen.
> But let justice roll down like waters,
>   and righteousness like an ever-flowing stream [5:21–24].

The New Testament hammers home the theme that indifference to poverty is a sign of misguided spirituality. Jesus told the religious leaders of his time:

> Woe to you, scribes and Pharisees, hypocrites! for you tithe mint and dill and cummin, and have neglected the weightier matters of the law, justice and mercy and faith; these you ought to have done, without neglecting the others. You blind guides, straining out a gnat and swallowing a camel! [Matt. 23:23–24].

The letter of James stresses the interrelationship between faith and concrete action that responds to the needs of the poor:

> What good is it to profess faith without practicing it? Such faith has no power to save one, has it? If a brother or sister has nothing to wear and no food for the day, and you say to them, "Good-bye and good luck! Keep warm and well fed," but do not meet their bodily needs, what good is that? So it is with the faith that does nothing in practice. It is thoroughly lifeless [2:14–17, NAB].

The problem is not that tithing, or prayer, or hymns of praise, or statements of faith are unimportant. The problem is that they are disconnected from God if they are disconnected from the reality of human suffering. Why? Because when humans suffer, God suffers. Elie Wiesel captures the power of this statement in an account of the execution of Jews in Nazi Germany:

> The three victims mounted together onto the chairs. The three necks were placed at the same moment within the nooses. "Long live liberty!" cried the two adults. But the child was silent.

"Where is God? Where is God?" someone behind me asked. At a sign from the head of the camp, the three chairs tipped over. Total silence throughout the camp. On the horizon, the sun was setting. . . .

Then the march past again. The two adults were no longer alive. Their tongues hung swollen, blue-tinged. But the third rope was still moving; being so light, the child was still alive. . . . For more than half an hour he stayed there, struggling between life and death, dying in slow agony under our eyes. And we had to look him full in the face. He was still alive when I passed in front of him. His tongue was still red, his eyes were not yet glazed.

Behind me, I heard the same man asking: "Where is God now?" And I heard a voice within me answer him: "Where is God? Here God is—God is hanging here on this gallows."[14]

We are told in Matthew 25 that when we feed or ignore the hungry, we feed or ignore Jesus. The tragedy of our faith and of the social organization of our lives is that we have the capacity to cut ourselves off from the poor. We are often so removed from the poor that we do not have to look them "full in the face." We do not see a relationship between their suffering and our lifestyles and economy.

A simple example can illustrate the problem. When we purchase bananas in a grocery store, most of us know little or nothing about the international economy and the companies that set the price for bananas, the control of shipping, landownership patterns in the exporting country, political repression (often supported by U.S. guns and dollars), the illnesses of banana workers and their families due to the use of pesticides produced in the U.S.A. (banned for use here and yet routinely exported), or the malnutrition that takes the lives of nearly half the children. Cutting ourselves off from the poor has dramatic *economic* consequences.

But the problem goes deeper. We have given little thought to the *spiritual* consequences of isolating ourselves from the poor and therefore cutting ourselves off from God. This does not mean that the poor are always godlike: anyone who romanticizes either poverty or the poor has experienced little of the reality of poverty. However, great religious leaders of recent history, including the prophets Mahatma Gandhi, Martin Luther King, Jr., Dorothy Day, and Oscar Romero, came to know God through their struggles *with* the poor and *against* the forces that oppress them.

Is our faith journey on the right track? Is it leading us in the direction God wants us to take? Does the theology of our churches have integrity? These are weighty questions that demand both discernment and humility. The situation of the poor and our relationship with them is a biblical guideline that can help us. Churches and communities of faith everywhere should be encouraged to examine their sermons, liturgies, hymnals, budgets, social involvement, investments, prayers, and educational programs in light of their relationship and relevancy to the poor.

God's Love Has Consequences

A common image of God is that of an otherworldly entity who helps us pass from this life to the next. Religion takes on the character of an after-life insurance policy. Hunger, poverty, and economic exploitation are not seen as related to salvation or spiritual health. God is banished from history and Christians close their eyes to their potentials and responsibilities.

This image contrasts sharply with the biblical God who is made known to human beings in the midst of their daily struggles. God looks for, longs for, works and suffers for justice and reconciliation within history. In this context, hunger and poverty are scandalous signs of sinfulness. They reflect problems of economic injustice and spiritual brokenness.

God's love is present wherever there is confrontation with and healing of this sinfulness. God's love is expressed through the compassionate actions of individuals and groups. Hearts that have grown hard or calloused by greed, pain, or despair are softened by God's transforming love. In this way individuals and communities of faith become co-workers with God in a ministry of healing, reconciliation, and justice.

A number of examples from scripture illustrate that God cares deeply about human history and not simply about a heavenly kingdom or reward at the end of history:

• The exodus story describes an oppressed and landless people groaning under its bondage and crying out. God hears the cry. God does not promise to take the Hebrews away to heaven but to deliver them from bondage and lead them to a land of plenty (Exod. 2:23; 3:7–8).

• God enters human history in the person of Jesus. This is the meaning of the incarnation. It would be difficult to imagine a greater commitment to the human person, to history, and to the created order than God's willingness to live, work, and die with and for us. Jesus taught that the kingdom of God was breaking *into history* in a new and decisive way (Matt. 4:23) and that we could experience, know, and serve God as we feed the hungry (Matt. 25:44–45). Jesus also taught us to pray: "Thy kingdom come, Thy will be done, *on earth* as it is in heaven" (Matt. 6:10; italics added).

• The ministry of Jesus is filled with examples of healing, compassion, and wholeness. Shortly before John the Baptist is killed, he sends his disciples to Jesus to ask if Jesus is the messiah. Jesus answers them, "Go and tell John what you hear and see: the blind receive their sight and the lame walk, lepers are cleansed and the deaf hear, and the dead are raised up, and the poor have good news preached to them" (Matt. 11:4–5). Throughout his ministry Jesus identifies historical healings and empowerment of the poor with God's kingdom and with manifestations of God's love.

• God's love has power to transform persons. Zacchaeus is a different person and has a radically different relationship with the poor after his encounter with Jesus. Mary Magdalene, the disciples, and others experience God's love in ways that enable them to become instruments of God's healing and compassion. Biblical themes such as repentance, conversion, and baptism reinforce an understanding of faith that involves transformation here and now. Repent and be converted from selfishness to sharing, from despair to hope, from hardheartedness to compassion, from unjust wealth to a commitment to the poor. Christian baptism has practical, historical consequences. It symbolizes the death of our old selves and our rebirth into a faith community that seeks to embody kingdom values (love, hope, compassion, equality, justice, and peace) within history. This rebirth within history, which was so confusing to Nicodemus (John 3:1-6), is made possible by God's love. It frees us to proclaim this love and to bring kingdom values to bear on all aspects of life.

If we are to be freed from our bondage to a hunger-perpetuating theology, then we must embrace a God who cares about history and a role for ourselves as persons immersed in history. This will involve a deeper understanding of sin, redemption, and salvation.

There are two common ways in which sin is talked about in the church: as a matter of personal morality and as an abstract part of human nature. In the first case we are told to lead exemplary *personal* lives. In the second case we remove ourselves from responsibility for social problems. "We are sinful, therefore hunger and poverty will always be with us." Individual morality is important, and understanding the depth of human sin can encourage social reformers to balance ideals with humility and realism. However, the biblical writers go beyond personal morality and abstract sin. They speak to *the disastrous consequences of personal complicity with social sin.* They understand that sin becomes embodied in social systems and economic relationships, and that this has material and spiritual implications for individuals and communities.

Christian complicity with social sin is reinforced by religion that keeps its distance from history, politics, and economics. A high-ranking U.S. government official at a Central American embassy told a group I was with that he was a good Christian. He then went on to say that there was no way to justify the U.S. policy of using Honduras as a base from which to overthrow the Sandinista government in Nicaragua. We asked how he as a Christian could carry out a policy he deemed totally indefensible. "Oh, that's easy," he replied. "My faith has nothing to do with my job. My job is to carry out the foreign policy of the United States. I can't let Christian faith speak to the morality of my job or I'd have to quit. It's best to keep these things separate." The separation of faith from our jobs, history, and economics clearly has devastating implications for the individuals involved—in this case, for the poor of Nicaragua, who are the victims of U.S.-sponsored aggression.

It may be that ultimately God's love and grace will prevail over all historical divisions. If final judgments before God are based on justice rather than mercy, most of us will be in trouble. However, *although God forgives sins, we live with the historical consequences of our actions.* For example, if I shoot and kill you with a gun, God may forgive my sin but you are dead. In a similar way, God

may forgive us for lifestyles that depend on the exploi
our direct or indirect support of repressive government
that victimize the poor. We may ultimately be forgi
problem of hunger remains or intensifies because of o
as we affirm the primacy of God's unconditional lov
scriptural testimony that *God's love and grace seek t*
actions that result in healings and redemptions within
the biblical writers to personal complicity with social sin is a call to conversion,
not resignation, *not* despair, *not* a withdrawal from history, politics, or economics, *not* a retreat into the safety of an afterlife, but conversion and reconciliation within history.

We can cling to wealth, power, and privilege and ignore the hungry. We can harden our hearts and distance ourselves from the poor— and in doing so isolate ourselves from God. We can distort theology to justify disengagement rather than involvement with the world. We can carry out and remain silent about foreign policies that are unjust and inflict misery on others. It may even be that we can do all these things with the assurance of God's forgiveness. However, we cannot do these things *with God's blessing* and we cannot do them without painful historical repercussions including hunger, poverty, violence, social turmoil, and spiritual decay.

Human history is the arena in which Christians live out their response to God's love. It is imperative, therefore, that we try to understand the world in which we live, including the obstacles to economic and spiritual health. In this context, it is absurd to say that politics and social analysis do not belong in the church. Tell it to Jesus and the prophets! Their understanding of the social nature of sin shaped their fostering of compassionate action. Isaiah and Amos condemned sinful social structures that resulted in the exploitation of the poor, the loss of land by small landholders, and the concentration of land in the hands of the rich, including bankers and grain merchants (Isa. 5:8; Amos 8:1–8). In their view, social sin embodied in unjust economic relationships made spiritual health impossible. Jesus detected the economic and religious idolatry of the money changers at the temple and he took appropriate action (Matt. 21:12–13). His actions and teachings on wealth and poverty flowed from his experience and understanding of the economic and spiritual costs of inequality and injustice.

The faith and theology of Jesus and the prophets showed deep levels of political awareness. They entered religious, political, and economic arenas as seekers of justice determined to put an end to the spiritual and economic burdens of oppression and poverty. Their faith, theology, and actions were shaped by their experiences of God's love and their understanding of social sin. The implications for us are clear. God's involvement in history, including a profound commitment to the liberation of rich and poor alike, points the way toward responsible Christian involvement.

Theology may be neutral in the sense that telling voters they will go to hell if they vote for a certain candidate is inappropriate. But theology always has al ramifications: it either illuminates or ignores the evil present in unjust ical and economic structures. Oscar Romero said at a Lenten service:

> Whoever believes that my preaching is political, that it provokes violence, as if I were the cause of all the evils in the republic, forgets that the word of the Church is not inventing the evils which already exist in the world, but illuminating them. The light illumines what already exists. It doesn't create it. The great evil already exists, and the word of God wants to do away with those evils. It points them out as part of a necessary denunciation so that people can return to good paths.[15]

God's word illuminates the darkness and identifies specific areas in need of reconciliation. God's love calls us to confront the darkness through compassionate action. Confrontation reduces the power that darkness has to control our lives and opens us to the possibility of healing and transformation. Our willingness to confront the darkness of social sin is related to our capacity for hope. Hunger, poverty, injustice, greed, selfishness, and violence lead many Christians to abandon possibilities for confrontation or transformation. The result is a deep cynicism that puts a straitjacket on both God and us. Often our desire is to escape the world rather than to confront or transform it. This desire is reinforced by a theology that constricts the biblical message to the security of an afterlife guaranteed by God.

Theology that downplays God's commitment to historical justice and discourages Christian involvement in the world distorts salvation and redemption. A redemptive theology overcomes cynicism and opens us to the possibility of God's transforming love. Salvation refers to the passage from death to life. However, the passage from death to life does not refer simply to the resurrection that follows physical death. It refers also to conversion and repentance within history.

It is true in a final sense that we do not save ourselves by our own actions; salvation is a gift of God's grace. However, we do participate in salvific works with God. *We experience salvation whenever the values of the kingdom challenge or overcome darkness.* Compassionate actions are salvific in the sense that they bring wholeness to situations that demand reconciliation and healing. The reconciliation between Zacchaeus and the defrauded brought salvation to his house. Conversely, James says that salvation is blocked when we utter words of comfort to the hungry or ill-clad *without* a compassionate response to their *physical* needs.

The biblical understanding of suffering can also help us to overcome cynicism and take up compassionate action. The biblical writers view suffering under two aspects: suffering that is imposed and suffering that is redemptive. Hunger, poverty, and illness that result from greed, indifference, and economic injustice are examples of imposed suffering. God hates the suffering that one person imposes on another. God's call to conversion is a call to terminate such suffering. *Redemptive* suffering is related to compassionate actions that have redeeming value. The supreme example of redemptive suffering is that of the crucified Jesus. Jesus' willingness to live out his mission, even to the point of death on a cross, unmasks the power of death. Death has no ultimate claim, because Jesus does not allow fear of death to prevent him from living faithfully, speaking the truth, challenging religious and political authorities, preaching the good news to the poor. Jesus' death also has redeeming value because through his suffering our sins are forgiven. The assurance of forgiveness frees us for involvement. We are called to take up our cross (Luke 9:23–25) and to risk redemptive suffering as we seek to overcome the personal and social causes of imposed suffering.

Redemptive actions resist evil, embody hope, promote healing, and testify to truth—despite the high personal costs that may be exacted. Oscar Romero understood that by standing with the poor in El Salvador he would have to share in their suffering:

> Christ invites us not to have fear of persecution, because—believe this, brothers and sisters—the one who is committed to the poor must experience the destiny of the poor. And in El Salvador we know the destiny of the poor: to disappear, to be tortured, to be captured, to have the appearance of a cadaver.[16]

As stated earlier, one biblical criterion by which we can judge the integrity of our faith is our relationship to the poor. Our proximity to a redemptive cross may be another criterion. Archbishop Romero understood that if he was to be killed, his death would be used by God for redemptive purposes. Fifteen days before his death he told a Guatemalan journalist in a confidential telephone conversation:

> I have frequently been threatened with death. I must tell you that, as a Christian, I do not believe in death without resurrection: if I am killed, I will rise again in the Salvadoran people. I say this to you without arrogance; I say it with the greatest humility.
>
> As a pastor, I am obliged, by divine command, to give my life for those whom I love—all Salvadorans, even those who may assassinate me. If the threat should come to pass, I offer God, from this very moment, my blood for the redemption and resurrection of El Salvador. . . . Martyrdom is a grace from God that I do not believe myself worthy of. But if God accepts the sacrifice of my life, may my blood be the seed of freedom and the sign that hope will soon become a reality. . . .
>
> May my death, if it is accepted by God, be for the liberation of my people and a testimony of hope in the future. You may say, if they should succeed in killing me, that I will forgive and bless those who will do it. I do wish, yes, that they might be convinced that they will be wasting their time: a bishop will die, but the church of God, which is the people, will never perish.[17]

God's love, alive in the hearts of the zealous, enters sinful situations as a force for compassion, hope, and justice. This love is sometimes put to the test. But it cannot be defeated: its refusal to be bound by death and injustice plants seeds that take root in the boundless determination of others.

When Christians become channels for kingdom values within history, they do not eliminate greed, hunger, or economic injustice. They do not create perfect societies or perfect economies or the full realization of the kingdom of God on earth. They do or can make life and economies *more* just, *more* compassionate, *more* hopeful. They see to it that social sins such as hunger and poverty are always met with confrontation and resistance rather than resignation.

God's love has historical consequences for the world and for the lives and actions of persons of faith. If our faith and our theology discourage involvement with the poor, stifle rather than encourage faith journeys, imprison rather than unleash hope, or encourage resignation rather than involvement, then they must be rejected as unbiblical and dangerous. The God of history offers us the gift of new life that enables us to participate in historical undertakings of healing, compassion, and justice.

The Integrity of Economic Priorities and Systems

On a trip to Iowa I met an economist who worked for a large agricultural machinery manufacturer. He spoke about the need to eliminate more family farms and about the "value-free" marketplace as offering the best hope for justice. He went on to say that wearing out the soil is no different from wearing out a house. Money will move to where it is most profitable and someday it may be profitable to restore the health of the soil.

The farmers and seminary professors who heard his talk disagreed with most of what this economist said. I told him about my concern that the greatest threat to national and global security is shortsighted economic policies that are undermining the sustention of the U.S. food system. His value-free marketplace was resulting in concentrated landownership, the decay of rural communities, and irreversible loss of prime farmland through erosion and urban encroachment. I recounted statistics to the effect that the U.S.A. loses 220 acres of farmland every hour to townhouses, shopping centers, highways, and coal mines, and how each day twenty-six square miles of topsoil wash and blow away from the farmland that remains.[18] He responded to my comments by saying that economists often disagree with theologians. In other words, economics is a specialized field that is best left to professional economists.

There are theological and practical reasons for *not* leaving economics solely to economists. On the practical side, the failure of traditional economics to address the problem of widespread hunger makes our questioning imperative. A value-free economics that creates profuse misery alongside coddled gluttony betrays fundamental weaknesses. The Bible refuses to separate economic and spiritual issues. Economic injustice has both material and spiritual consequences.

The Bible is not a treatise in economics. It does not tell us exactly how to
organize an economy, nor does it provide specific solutions to complex present-
day economic problems. However, it does provide a simple criterion by which
we can judge the integrity of economic priorities and systems: *the well-being of
the poor.* The basis of "biblical economics" is a logic of sufficiency for the
poor, what I will refer to from this point on as "the logic of the majorities." The
biblical writers suggest that the integrity of economic systems and priorities can
be measured by assessing our relationship to the poor and their well-being.

There are three important biblical insights that can illuminate the relationship between economic justice and spiritual health. First, *it is the situation of
the poor, not the well-being of the rich, that determines the legitimacy of an
economy.* The rich in Israel at the time of Amos would reverse the terms of this
principle. They look to the affluence. Amos as God's messenger looks to the
suffering of the poor.

The drama unfolds in Amos 6:1–6. In the first verse Amos proclaims God's
judgment:

> Woe to the complacent in Zion,
> > to the overconfident on the mount of Samaria.
> Leaders of a nation favored from the first,
> > to whom the people of Israel have recourse! [NAB].

Amos records the response of the upper classes in the second verse. They tell
him to compare the prosperity of Israel with that of surrounding nations.
Surely Amos can admit the absurdity of questioning the economic or religious
life of Israel! They say to him:

> Pass over to Calneh and see,
> > go from there to Hamath the great,
> > and down to Gath of the Philistines!
> Are you better than these kingdoms,
> > or is your territory wider than theirs? [NAB].

Amos speaks of them in verses 4–6:

> Lying upon beds of ivory,
> > stretched comfortably on their couches,
> they eat lambs taken from the flock,
> > and calves from the stall!
> Improvising to the music of the harp,
> > like David, they devise their own accompaniment.

> They drink wine from bowls,
> and anoint themselves with the best oils;
> yet they are not made ill by the collapse
> of Joseph [i.e., Israel] [NAB].

⊥nis story in Amos is that of the age-old confrontation between the logic of the majorities and the logic of wealth and power. The rich in Israel see their wealth as evidence that Amos is a false prophet. Wealth is a powerful and arrogant symbol of the viability of their economy and their faith. God through Amos announces that it is poverty and economic exploitation that shape one's judgment about the legitimacy of an economy. An economy that enriches a minority while brutalizing the majority is condemned.

A second important insight is the stress of the biblical writers on equity *as a foundation for a just economy and for spiritual health*. The principal wealth-producing resource in biblical times is land. Every fifty years this precious resource is to be redistributed in order to correct inequalities that develop over time (Lev. 25:10). The theological principle that undergirds this year of jubilee is that God owns the land. The land is meant to be a blessing to all its inhabitants; those who work it are stewards, caretakers of a gift, sojourners with God (Lev. 25:23). Amos and Isaiah condemn the concentration of land-holdings that results in economic injustice and spiritual brokenness (Amos 5; Isa. 3:12-15; 5:8-10). Jesus defines his ministry in terms of good news to the poor and liberty to the oppressed—and the acceptable year of the Lord (a probable reference to the jubilee year, Luke 4:18-19).

The sabbatical provisions provide further testimony to the importance of equity to economics. Every seventh year is to be a sabbatical year in which debts are forgiven, Hebrew slaves freed, and the land allowed to lie fallow in order to have its fertility restored (Deut. 15:1-6, 12-18; Lev. 25:2-7). The biblical legislators assume that economic systems will eventually give rise to inequalities in wealth and power. The way to prevent this, or lessen its impact, is to institutionalize mechanisms that break the cycle of poverty and return productive resources to the people. Land reforms and cancelation of debt are examples of such mechanisms.

A third biblical insight is that *the goal and expectation for an economy is sufficiency, not affluence*. Sufficiency is a precondition for spiritual health. Affluence is a prescription for economic and spiritual disaster because it almost always depends on the denial of sufficiency for some in order to satisfy the greed of others.

Sufficiency and willingness to accept limits are consistent themes within scripture. God provides the people in the wilderness with manna and yet what they gather beyond daily need spoils (Exod. 16:17-21). Jesus transforms a little food into sufficiency for all in the stories of the feeding of the "five thousand men, besides women and children" (Matt. 14:15-21; Mark 6:30-44; Luke 9:10-17; John 6:1-13). "Give us *this day* our daily bread" is part of the prayer our Lord taught us to pray (Matt. 6:11; italics added).

The early church described in the Acts of the Apostles is a community in which "all who believed were together and had all things in common; and they sold their possessions and goods and distributed them to all, as any had need" (2:44–45). Paul implores churches having more to share with those having less: "I do not mean that others should be eased and you burdened, but that as a matter of equality your abundance at the present time should supply their want, so that their abundance may supply your want, that there may be equality" (2 Cor. 8:13–14). The spiritual consequences of failing to set limits and accept sufficiency for all as the goal of economic life are clear in the following biblical passages:

> Give me neither poverty nor riches; feed me with the food that is needful for me, lest I be full, and deny thee, and say, "Who is the Lord?" or lest I be poor, and steal, and profane the name of my God [Prov. 30:8–9].

> For we brought nothing into the world, and we cannot take anything out of the world; but if we have food and clothing, with these we shall be content. But those who desire to be rich fall into temptation, into a snare, into many senseless and hurtful desires that plunge people into ruin and destruction. For the love of money is the root of all evils; it is through this craving that some have wandered away from the faith and pierced their hearts with many pangs [1 Tim. 6:7–10].

Sufficiency should be the hallmark of a Christian lifestyle. Sufficiency linked to the biblical mandates of equity and justice reflects essential elements of the logic of the majorities. This logic of the majorities provides a solid foundation from which to critique the problem of world hunger, the political and economic crises in Central America, and the arms race.

SUMMARY

A liberating theology frees us to be agents of hope, healing, and compassion. It affirms God's profound commitment to creation, to history, and to reconciliation and justice among all persons and peoples. It acknowledges the reality of personal and social sin without denying the possibilities of God's transforming love. It rejoices in God's unconditional love even as it testifies to God's hatred of injustice and God's desire for historical healing and reconciliation.

A liberating theology moves beyond the problem of works/righteousness, leaves final judgments to God, and encourages believers to work for the historical healings between rich and poor on which economic and spiritual health depend. It moves beyond cynicism and despair to compassionate action rooted in Christ's example of redemptive suffering. It refuses to romanticize poverty and yet clearly states that our isolation from the poor reinforces economic injustice and prevents us from knowing God. It affirms the importance of belief but links belief to our willingness to embark upon a journey with

God at the center of our lives. It acknowledges diversity within scripture and yet sets out guidelines that can help Christians and their communities of faith to assess the authenticity of faith journeys and economic life.

Our firmest foundation for a liberating theology is the sure knowledge that the God who loves us enough to disrupt our lives travels with us as we journey.

Chapter 3

World Hunger and
the Logic of the Majorities

A group of Christians from the U.S.A. heard about the worsening problem of hunger and poverty in Guatemala. They went to a wise teacher and asked her: "How can we show compassion to hungry persons in Guatemala?" She told them a parable:

"There was a Christian family who went to church each Sunday, prayed daily, and studied the Bible regularly. They heard about hunger in Guatemala but they were too busy with their religious life to respond. The Guatemalans remained hungry.

"Another Christian heard about the hungry Guatemalans and faithfully included them in her prayers. The Guatemalans appreciated those prayers but they still lacked basic foods and their children's bellies swelled for lack of nourishment.

"Several business executives with money and impressive stock portfolios were deeply concerned when they heard about the plight of the Guatemalans. They made tax-deductible monthly pledges to a Guatemalan relief and development agency. However, they canceled their pledges when the agency spoke out against the labor practices of a company in which they had major investments. Employees received less than a minimum wage and their children received less than the minimal daily requirements of calories and protein.

"A pastoral team from a large church spoke with a woman who had recently returned from Guatemala. But they decided not to burden their congregation with this issue, because it was too controversial. Their church was in the middle of a fund-raising drive to pay for a new Sunday school wing and a new organ. A Guatemalan priest she knew, who ministered to the poor, was assassinated after he preached a sermon calling for land reform and other basic human rights.

"A retired general, president of his local congregation, dropped a check in the mail for Guatemalan relief on his way to testify to a congressional hearing on military assistance to Guatemala. He spoke in favor of increased weapons sales and aid to an admittedly repressive and brutal government because it was fighting communism. The Guatemalans remained hungry and if they protested their situation they were brutally tortured.

"A woman who was active in the social concerns committee of her church was filled with compassion when she heard about the situation of hunger in Guatemala. She organized a fund raiser for Guatemalan relief and development. She also encouraged her church to become a sanctuary for Central American refugees, lobbied government officials to block military aid to Guatemala, participated in demonstrations, and withheld a percentage of her income tax as a protest against U.S. support of a repressive government. Guatemalans received food and medical supplies, and they were filled with hope at the persistence of this woman as she challenged the politics of hunger.

"Who showed compassion to hungry Guatemalans?" the teacher asked.

THE LOGIC OF THE MAJORITIES

A graphic sign of the death of compassion is the relative silence on world hunger. One reason for widespread silence is that discussions about hunger are often very technical. Complex factor is built upon complex factor until solutions seem impossible. Complexity muddles understanding until the safest course of action seems to be inaction—and indifference triumphs again.

Hunger is complex inasmuch as study of it leads to an examination of a variety of personal and social issues. But this complexity need not be discouraging. Many of the causes of hunger are relatively easy to identify. Although lasting solutions are difficult to project, it is possible to discover avenues for compassionate action. We can identify and work for necessary changes in our personal lives and conduct, in the theology and life of our churches, and in the economic and foreign policies of our nation. Our lifestyles, economics, foreign trade, military policies, and biblical faith can be challenged by hunger-related concerns.

Biblical economics is focused on sufficiency, equity, and the well-being of the poor—the logic of the majorities. I shall argue that within the international economy and most national economies there is a nearly total disregard for the biblical logic of the majorities and that this disregard for biblical principles results in widespread injustice and hunger. For example:

• The biblical writers see land as a gift of God to the whole human family, and they promote periodic redistribution of this wealth-producing resource. Today land and other wealth-producing resources are concentrated in the hands of a few.

- The biblical writers promote cancelation of debt as a mechanism to break cycles of poverty. Today indebtedness is both a consequence and a tool of exploitation.
- According to the biblical logic of the majorities, the U.S. and world economy should be judged in relation to domestic and world hunger and poverty. Instead, the rich judge economic systems in light of their experience of affluence.
- The biblical logic of the majorities stipulates that economic choices should be biased in favor of the poor. Economists today promote a so-called value-free economics that is generally biased against the poor and reinforces the power of the rich.
- The biblical emphasis on sufficiency, equity, and the well-being of the poor raises serious questions about the nature and workings of capitalism. However, capitalism has taken on the appearance of a god that is rarely questioned.

In addition to these clashes between the biblical logic of the majorities and present-day economic values and priorities, the following commonsense observations on the causes of hunger should be kept in mind. They will be elaborated on in both this chapter and the next:

- You can live in a rich country and still be hungry.
- If you have a lot of land or money, you probably eat well.
- The wealthy associate with the wealthy; they have little or no personal experience of the living conditions of the poor.
- If powerful individuals or groups make money doing things that cause hunger for others, they will continue doing so until their power is effectively challenged.
- If other powerful individuals and groups provide weapons to the powerful groups who make money while causing hunger then they will continue doing so longer.
- Indebtedness may be hazardous to your health.
- International trade is like an unequal boxing match: a 165-pound weakling (like me) will get clobbered if forced to box a world heavyweight champion.
- If dehumanizing labels are applied to individuals or groups, it is easier to kill them or tolerate their being killed.
- The problem of hunger will not be solved through the production and consumption of video games.
- People don't like being hungry or oppressed.
- Dollars and cents often muddle common sense.

GUATEMALA—"A BUSINESSMAN'S DREAM"

In the spring of 1982, CBS News presented a documentary entitled "Central America in Revolt." It included a segment on Guatemala that candidly addressed many of the causes of hunger. It was particularly relevant for U.S. citizens because it highlighted the relationship between hunger, repression, and social upheaval, on the one hand, and U.S. corporate and governmental policies on the other. It was also useful for Christians living in the U.S.A. because it graphically illustrated how a total disregard for the biblical logic of the majorities is at the root of the world food crisis, and how social systems can impede or enhance our capacity to be compassionate.

CBS reporter Ed Rable painted the background to the Guatemalan scene. Guatemala is strategically the most important of all Central American nations. The U.S. State Department, according to Rable, sees it as "the prize of the region, the most cherished banana republic of them all." It is five times the size of El Salvador and is rich in natural resources including oil. Guatemala has enough oil to meet "up to 10 percent of U.S. needs." It is the most populous and industrialized of the Central American nations with what Rable referred to as "a large, cheap labor force" that has attracted "sizeable U.S. investments." One hundred ninety U.S. corporations do business in Guatemala, forty-four "are *Fortune 500* blue-chip giants."

The CBS documentary went on to describe one of the significant events in the history of Guatemala. In 1954, a CIA-backed coup ousted the democratically elected reformist government headed by Jacobo Arbenz Guzmán. Arbenz had offended the U.S.-based United Fruit Company (now United Brands) with his land reform program. His ouster, according to Rable, marked "the end of democracy." In 1955 Vice-President Nixon was sent to Guatemala to celebrate the successful coup. "Ever since," Rable commented, "power in Guatemala has stayed in the hands of an ultraconservative group of fat cats—wealthy landowners and industrialists friendly to American business interests—the legacy of '54."

CBS effectively portrayed Guatemala as many American business executives see it. It did so through the life and mind-set of Fred Sherwood. Fred Sherwood flew in the CIA airforce that toppled Arbenz in 1954. He has lived half his life in Guatemala and was once president of the American Chamber of Commerce there. He owns a rubber plantation and a cement factory, and he manages a textile mill. Ed Rable described Guatemala as a "businessman's dream." Profits are high. Costs are low. The following exchange took place at Sherwood's textile mill:

Sherwood: We have a large labor market and the workers are very good. You teach them and they don't mind doing the same thing day after day. . . . Americans like variation but here the people do the same thing day after day and they are very good.
Rable: Is the government pretty cooperative?
Sherwood: Oh yes! Very, very cooperative. We don't have restrictions as to environmental things and there [are] just no restrictions or rules at all. So that makes it nice.
Rable: Are the people here oppressed in any way?
Sherwood: I don't think so really. I don't think so. I know of no individual, I know of no one. I've lived here for thirty-six years. I've been in farming, in industry and commerce, and I don't know anybody being

[oppressed]. No one forces them to do anything. I think this is just something some reporters have thought up.

Almost anyone who travels to Guatemala or other parts of Central America knows that oppression is not the invention of journalists. Guatemala, the "businessman's dream," is a nightmare for the vast majority of its citizens. The CBS documentary reported that 2 percent of the population owns 70 percent of the land, 70 percent of the population lives on $74 a year, half the population can neither read nor write, and the infant mortality rate is the highest in Central America.

Many Guatemalans are working to change present injustices. However, according to Rable, those who seek change are regarded as "threats to the economic status quo and considered communist enemies of the state." Fifty to sixty political murders occur each day. "Priests, nuns, journalists, labor leaders, teachers, students, and peasants are among the dead. Opposition political leaders are particularly hard hit."

Fred Sherwood saw a different Guatemala:

Rable: I want to ask you a question about something a politician here in this country told me. He said that more than one hundred twenty of his party's leaders had been assassinated in about an eighteen-month period. I'm just wondering what you make of that kind of statement.

Sherwood: Well, in the first place I'd very much question it because I don't think there's been one hundred and twenty people of all types assassinated here in the last year. *I mean I'm not counting the peasants or men of that category.* No, I think that's probably exaggerated to a great extent. There were a couple of politicians assassinated a couple of years ago but believe me they were way out in left field. These people, I think, are our enemies. They're against our way of life. Maybe assassination is not the right word for it but I don't think they should be allowed to run free to try to destroy our form of government—our way of life, in other words [italics added].

Guatemala is a "businessman's dream" in terms of high profits and governmental support of repressive, probusiness policies. It is a "businessman's dream" in another sense as well. Fred Sherwood's perspective on Guatemala is dreamlike. It is out of touch with the vast majority of Guatemalans. Such dreams are costly for the majority of Guatemalans who wake each morning to face a world of hunger and oppression. In order to defend another way of life, it is necessary for Fred Sherwood's allies to assassinate political leaders and professionals. Others, considered less than human, are murdered, but "they don't count."

HUNGER—A PROFITABLE ENTERPRISE

Guatemala is typical of countries where hunger is rampant. Unequal control and distribution of resources, political repression, self-justifying ideology, and sinister alliances between domestic and foreign business interests are nearly always present where there is hunger. Human hunger is neither an accident nor a historical necessity. It is often the direct or indirect result of the accumulation of wealth by individuals or groups at the expense of others. As Padre Pedro and the Salvadorans at the refugee cooperative understood, some persons like what Jesus does and others oppose his actions. Similarly, some individuals and groups affirm a biblical economics based on the logic of the majorities; others will do whatever they must to ensure their own power and privilege.

Simply stated, hunger is profitable. The policies that enrich some impoverish others. Condemnation of such policies goes back at least to the Old Testament prophets:

> The Lord enters into judgment
>   with the elders and princes of [the] people;
> "It is you who have devoured the vineyard,
>   the spoil of the poor is in your houses.
> What do you mean by crushing my people,
>   by grinding the face of the poor?"
>   says the Lord God of hosts [Isa. 3:14–15].

> Like a basket full of birds,
>   their houses are full of treachery;
> therefore they have become great and rich,
>   they have grown fat and sleek.
> They know no bounds in deeds of wickedness;
>   they judge not with justice
> the cause of the fatherless, to make it prosper,
>   and they do not defend the rights of the needy
>   [Jer. 5:27–28].

The houses, factories, plantations, bank accounts, and stock portfolios of the rich are full of treachery. They are financed by exploiting the labor of the poor or by squandering the resources that should be used to meet unmet needs rather than limitless greed. Consider the following insights from the CBS documentary:

- Hunger is a problem in countries that are rich in natural resources.
- Hunger is a by-product of rich agricultural land owned and controlled by a small minority.
- Foreign businesses and wealthy elites in underdeveloped countries form alliances that are mutually beneficial but victimize the poor.
- The poor are viewed at best as a supply of cheap labor. The outspoken poor or their advocates are considered communist subversives.
- U.S. foreign policy sees to it that alliances between local elites and U.S. businesses run smoothly. (This subject is taken up in chap. 4.)

Hunger and Natural Resources

It will be helpful to keep in mind three commonsense observations on hunger as the relationship between hunger and natural resources is explored: you can live in a rich country and be hungry; a nonathlete will be clobbered if forced to fight a world champion; and if you are in debt, you may be in trouble.

It seems strange at first that extensive hunger is common to many countries that are relatively well endowed with resources. There are two principal reasons for this paradox. First, *inequality and injustice within nations.* Inequality within nations is obvious to even the most casual observers. During the summer of 1983 my wife, Sara, and I lived in Mexico. We were struck by the affluence, opulence, and abundance of resources and goods nearly as much as we were alarmed by the poverty and degradation of the majority of Mexicans. Luxury alongside unmet needs is common in many countries with adequate resources. Basic human needs could be met but skewed priorities make hunger persistent and predictable. In the CBS documentary on Guatemala the lifestyle of the "ultaconservative group of fat cats" and their U.S. counterparts contrasts sharply with the 70 percent of Guatemalans who live on $74 a year.

A second reason for the paradox of hunger in the midst of adequate resources is *inequality and injustice between nations.* Inequality between nations is partly the result of differences in resource endowment (a problem to be discussed below). It is also a consequence of injustice that is built into the international trading system. The terms of trade from colonial times to the present have enriched the industrialized countries while impoverishing their trading partners in Africa, Asia, and Latin America. Underdevelopment in these countries is the direct result of their subservient relationship to the U.S.A. and Western Europe.

Pricing policies within the international economy are set on the basis of *the relative power of trading partners rather than on the basis of fairness measured by the ability to meet human needs.* Small countries such as El Salvador or Nicaragua are supposed to balance their power with that of the U.S.A. or Western Europe (or a block of developed countries) in ways that promote beneficial trade relationships. Advocates of "free trade" and a "free and open international economy" have a distorted understanding of freedom; it ignores the reality of unequal power relationships. The result of unequal power relationships between relatively rich and relatively poor countries is that poor countries, like the nonathlete forced to fight the world heavy-weight champion, get clobbered. Present international pricing and trade policies insure the continuous transfer of wealth from poor countries to the already rich.

Poor countries lack sufficient power to negotiate fair prices. Therefore, the prices they receive for exports of raw materials, minerals, and food stuffs have not kept pace with the costs of the goods they import. In 1970, for example, 100 pounds of coffee bought 100 barrels of oil; in 1982 they bought three barrels. In 1977, 4.4 tons of coffee bought a tractor; in 1982 the same tractor cost the equivalent of 11.2 tons, an increase of 145 percent.[19] A U.S. bipartisan commission reported in 1984 that "Central America would have to export in physical terms almost half again as much today as it did five years ago to buy the same goods on the world market."[20] Steep increases in oil prices have also hurt the underdeveloped countries lacking their own oil reserves. Industrialized nations have generally been able to pass the higher costs for oil to the ultimate purchasers of industrial products. Poor countries have been on the receiving end of these price increases at the same time that their export earnings have fallen. Also, underdeveloped countries that have diversified their exports to include manufactured goods face stiff tariffs and other import restrictions from the U.S.A. and Western Europe.

The result of these trends is that poor countries are faced with worsening poverty coupled with a massive and increasing debt burden. Latin American countries and other developing nations are so far in debt that there is little prospect of their making significant payments on the principal. Many countries are using substantial amounts of their GNP simply to pay the interest on their debts. Others are unable to meet interest payments.

Central America is suffocating in debt. In 1960 the external public debt of Central American countries was equivalent to 3 percent of their GNP. By 1970 it had risen to 8 percent, and by 1980 to 46 percent. In 1981 the external public debt of Central America totaled almost $11 billion—more than twice the value of its annual exports. A year later indebtedness topped $14 billion, a 240 percent increase over 1975. The debt of Central American countries increased forty-two times between 1960 and 1981.[21]

Indebtedness is the logical consequence of the dependent position of underdeveloped countries within the international economy. It is also a sign of their vulnerability, humiliation, and constriction within the worldwide system:

• *Indebtedness,* a consequence of exploitation within the international economy, *itself becomes a factor in further exploitation.* Indebtedness allows the U.S.A. to influence the economic policies of underdeveloped countries. The International Monetary Fund (IMF), an international financial institution that audits debtor countries and serves as a lender of last resort, is often in a position to dictate economic policy. Generally, the IMF requires drastic cuts in spending programs for the poor, wage reductions, and increased incentives for foreign business investment. The power of the IMF is enhanced by the fact that unless IMF conditions are met, countries cannot obtain loans from private banks, other multilateral development banks, or other governments. The practical result of IMF policies is to enhance the position of foreign investors while further aggravating the situation of the poor. The implementation of IMF policies is often followed by increased social turmoil (resistance to the imposition of greater hardships), which is often met by government repression. The U.S. verbal commitment to encourage political democracy is contradicted by the unswerving commitment to an international economy that spawns poverty, social turmoil, and political repression.

• *Indebtedness can lock countries into devastating economic patterns.* It is sometimes wondered why the ouster of a repressive government is not immediately followed by radical improvements in the well-being of a people. There are many answers to this question. Underdevelopment is deeply rooted, resources are limited, education and transportation systems may be undeveloped or inadequate, and the terms of trade remain skewed in favor of developed countries. Indebtedness imposes other limitations. For example, any country that wants to reorient its agricultural priorities in order to meet local food needs must balance this goal with the reality of a debt that often must be paid with revenues from agricultural exports.

• *Indebtedness,* along with various forms of military support and intervention, *has become a principal point of leverage by which the U.S.A. carries out its foreign policy goals.* For example, Honduras and Costa Rica have been of great importance in U.S. efforts to overthrow the Nicaraguan government. Their participation was secured in part because economic problems, including indebtedness, make them vulnerable to U.S. pressure. Jeane Kirkpatrick, while U.S. Ambassador to the United Nations, reportedly told Costa Rican officials not to expect substantial U.S. economic assistance until they built an army. (In May 1985, U.S. military advisors arrived in Costa Rica to begin training counterinsurgency battalions.)[22] Mexico, a country with a debt burden of more than $90 billion, has angered the U.S. government by pursuing an independent foreign policy in Central America. Mexico is under intense pressure to conform to U.S. plans for the region or face a tightening of U.S. purse strings.

• *Ironically, indebtedness is both a result of injustice within the international economy and a potential weapon to be used by underdeveloped countries in demanding a new international economic order.* There is an emerging consensus among many underdeveloped countries that their debts are both unjust and unpayable. For example, by the middle of 1985 Latin American countries owed more than $360 billion. Many leaders within Latin America are growing impatient with an international economy that fosters ever-escalating debt burdens while demanding interest payments that are paid by sacrificing internal development and the needs of the poor. There is a growing sense of power in the knowledge that if one or more of the major debtor countries, such as Mexico, Brazil, or Argentina (or a coalition of smaller countries), were to refuse to pay its debts the international economy could collapse and many of the largest U.S.-based banks would be bankrupt. The debt crisis, therefore, could be the most significant international issue of the last half of the 1980s.

Inequality within and between nations involves a double jeopardy for the poor. Wealth is unequally distributed within countries, with the result that the luxury consumption of a rich minority contrasts sharply with the stark poverty of the majority. At the same time, the international economy robs poor countries of potential wealth through unfair trade practices. The resulting debt burden becomes a tool of exploitation that further victimizes the poor. The reality of mass hunger has done little to challenge the almost sacred character of the marketplace. However, to speak of a "free international economy" in the context of unequal wealth and power is to engage in a form of doublespeak. References to "freedom" serve as a cover for an international system that is little more than a crude form of survival of the fittest based on power rather than compassion. This system condemns the poor to perpetual misery and dependency. The international economy, neither free nor magical, causes hunger and blocks compassion.

Hunger and Landownership

One would have a hard time imagining a situation more distant from the biblical logic of the majorities than present landownership and use patterns. The World Bank estimates that in eighty-three countries 3 percent of the population owns or controls 80 percent of the arable land.[23] A commonsense observation cited earlier suggests that this 3 percent, along with other monied elites, probably eat well. A corollary to this observation is that if you are not a large landowner and if you do not have money, you probably are hungry. There are no better statistics than those from the World Bank to help someone understand hunger and social turmoil in underdeveloped countries.

Land is central to the production of new wealth. It is vital to economic security and well-being everywhere, particularly in countries where populations are predominantly rural. When land is owned and controlled by a powerful minority, recent history has taught us to expect political and economic oppression, a mass exodus from rural to urban areas, and widespread social unrest.

Why is land so central to understanding hunger and social change movements? The answer can be found by breaking this question into two related parts. First, *What are production priorities when a powerful minority owns or controls the land?* This question leads to a curious paradox. Many countries with severe hunger problems utilize much of their best land for the production of agricultural products for export. Most of these exports end up on the tables of those who are already overfed in Western Europe and the United States. Half of Central American agricultural land is devoted to agro-exports.[24]

Landed elites make decisions about what they produce and where to market their products, based on profitability. Within the present international division of labor this generally means production and export of coffee, tea, cocoa, bananas, rubber, and other nonessential agricultural commodities. Nutritious foods are also produced—and exported. If poverty restricts a national market, there are often international consumers willing to pay. Honduras, Mexico, Guatemala, Haiti, and other poor countries help make the U.S.A. the largest importer of beef in the world. Mexico, where millions know hunger as a constant companion, supplies U.S. consumers with one-half to two-thirds of many fresh vegetables that they consume during the winter and spring.[25]

The second important question related to land has to do with *victims and beneficiaries.* Export agriculture is not a bad thing per se. Agricultural exports can earn the foreign exchange that poor countries need for development. The question is, development for whom? In 1929, Alberto Masferrer, a prominent Salvadoran journalist, teacher, and diplomat, warned of the victimization of the poor that accompanied the expansion of export agriculture:

> The conquest of territory by the coffee industry is alarming. It has occupied the highlands and is now descending to the valleys, displacing maize, rice, and beans. It has extended like the conquistador, spreading hunger and misery. Although it is possible to prove mathematically that these changes make the country richer, in fact they mean death.
>
> It is true that the cost of importing maize is small in relation to the benefits of the export of coffee, but is the imported grain given to the poor? Or must they pay for it? Is the income of the *campesino* who has lost his land adequate to provide maize, rice, and beans? Medicine and doctors? What good does it do to make money from the sale of coffee when it leaves so many in misery? *[La Patria].*

The control and use of land determines whether agriculture serves the interests of the vast majority of a national population or the interests of elites. Who benefits and who loses when landed elites stress export production over local needs? There are four groupings of gainers and losers:

• Large landowners are the most obvious beneficiaries. Export agriculture is profitable for the 2 percent of the landholders who own 60 percent of the land in El Salvador, and for the landed elites in Guatemala and elsewhere. They use some of their profits from exports to buy domestically produced or imported foods and luxury goods priced well beyond the reach of the poor. They are full participants in the international economy, both as producers and as consumers.

• A second group that profits from export agriculture comprises the foreign corporations that process, transport, or market export crops. Corporations such as General Foods or United Brands form strategic alliances with large producers. The coupling of hunger and profitable corporate practices is sometimes bitterly ironic. For example, Brazil exports 97 percent of its orange crop to companies such as Coca-Cola, whereas U.S. soft drink companies vigorously market vast amounts of nonnutritious soft drinks in Brazil, many of whose inhabitants suffer severe vitamin C deficiency.[26]

• The benefits of export agriculture accrue to groups that profit from foreign imports or the production of luxury goods. This group includes wealthy consumers and domestic and foreign businesses. Export agriculture is the sector that earns the foreign exchange that finances imports. The problem is that imports are generally selected by the rich. It should not be surprising that imports usually focus on luxury consumer goods or the resources and materials necessary to produce them, and the military hardware that defends unjust privileges.

Brazil finances luxury imports and production with revenues from agricultural exports. It is the second largest exporter of agricultural commodities in the world and yet 50 percent of the Brazilian population is malnourished. Land once used by local growers to produce a protein staple such as black beans is now used by large landowners in conjunction with foreign companies to produce soybeans that end up in the stomachs of West European cattle.[27]

• The main victims of present landownership and use patterns are the poor majority. Their needs are ignored. Production priorities stress exports over local needs, and the benefits from exports accrue to large landowners, urban elites, and foreign companies.

UNHEALTHY ALLIANCES

You can live in a rich country and be hungry. Rich individuals and groups promote each others' interests. Production and consumption of video games will not end hunger. These are three commonsense observations that shed light on the problem of unhealthy alliances. It can be misleading to speak of rich and poor countries. There is significant hunger in the richest of countries and significant wealth in all but the poorest of countries.

In the interconnected world of today it is sometimes more enlightening to look at hunger in the context of an international economy that works well for some and not so well for others. The poor of the world, regardless of their homeland, are often victims of the international economy. The rich of the world, regardless of their homeland, are often the beneficiaries of that same economy.

The fact that there is an international economic linkage between rich and poor countries does not mean that all countries are equally endowed with resources. The resources available for development vary from country to country. They are a significant factor in determining the relative well-being or deprivation of national populations. For example, there is little comparison between the natural wealth of the United States and that of Somalia. It is also true that some countries are so poor that they could approximate perfect domestic justice and still be in need of dramatic improvements in the international economy and significant help from the international community in order to meet the basic needs of their peoples. Mechanisms for international sharing need to be created or improved in order to respond to such situations.

The fact that some countries are extremely poor should not divert attention from the ways in which the international economy is an obstacle to compassion, aggravating inequalities between rich and poor. One out of every seven persons in the U.S.A., a total of more than 30 million, live below the poverty line. One in seven U.S. children receives virtually no health care; one in three has never been to a dentist.[28] Guatemala is rich in land, resources, and oil; yet, according to the CBS documentary mentioned above, 70 percent of its people subsist on $74 a year. It would be difficult to link hunger in Guatemala or the

U.S.A. to absolute scarcity. Hunger is a consequence of economic inequality, skewed development priorities, and neglect. The international economy connects the rich and poor from these and other countries. It improves the lives of some and impoverishes others.

A farmer from the Philippines graphically explained to me what it means to say that the international economy is laced with sinister alliances. He and his family had farmed the same land for generations. A decision made hundreds of miles away changed their lives forever. The Filipino government decided to increase foreign exchange earnings by expanding agricultural exports. It sent in troops to remove inhabitants from a large tract of land that would soon be devoted to production of pineapples and bananas for export. The land was readied for production by bulldozers, which followed the troops and tore up the land. The farm families were evicted. Those who resisted were arrested, tortured, or killed. He himself had torture marks all over his hands and arms. His land, and that of his neighbors, ended up belonging to relatives of Filipino President Ferdinand Marcos, or under the jurisdiction of U.S.-based banana exporting companies.

He ended our conversation with a request that I return to the U.S.A. and tell the American people three things:

> First, tell your people that the U.S. is the largest area for missionary work in the world. Be missionaries to your own people because it is the theology of your churches that tolerates so much injustice. Second, tell them that we are more concerned about economic justice than foreign aid. Poverty in the Philippines is the result of ties between U.S. multinational companies and the wealthy sectors in my country. Finally, you must work with others to halt the flow of U.S. weapons which protect these unhealthy alliances but keep my people poor.

One of the most striking features of an international economy dominated by prejudicial alliances is how little of world productivity is geared to meeting basic human needs. The earth is extremely productive. The international production and distribution of goods is impressive. The world can appear to be an intricate, dynamic network of raw materials, resources, factories, and farms. The enormous amounts of nonrenewable resources that fuel this production and distribution seem wasteful, destructive, and shortsighted in terms of future needs. But the disregard for *future* generations is not nearly as striking as the disregard for *present* generations victimized by poverty. The unmet needs of more than a billion human beings contrast sharply with the widespread production, availability, and consumption of nonessential and even dangerous products.

An interesting experiment can be done with friends or family members. Each person should visit a variety of stores and make two lists. On one list write down all the items you consider basic or essential. On the other, list items you consider luxuries or nonessentials. Compare your lists with others. I think you will either be surprised by how many nonessentials crept onto your basic needs list or you will be shocked by the length of your list of luxuries and nonessentials.

My list of nonessentials would include high-fashion clothes; disposable items—cups, razors, diapers, and lighters; microwave ovens; war toys; cosmetics; highly processed foods; air conditioners; electric toothbrushes and blowdryers; video games; trash compactors; automatic dishwashers; electric garage-door openers. If we add to our list luxury automobiles and the petroleum products to run them, color television sets, video recorders, snowmobiles, and the like, it becomes more evident how our lifestyles waste precious resources.

Someone may object that life is more than simply meeting basic human needs. I agree. Life is more than basic food, clothing, shelter, education, and health care. There are varying interpretations as to what constitutes a basic need or a luxury. My point is that nearly one out of every four human beings lacks these basic needs. This is a fundamental distortion. Life *is* more than basic food, clothing, and shelter; however, the deprivation of these most basic needs for a quarter of humankind diminishes all of us both spiritually and economically.

The international economy is stoked by the corporate desire for profit and the purchasing power (money) of the rich. The de facto goal of economic development has little to do with making adequate provision for the world population. The goal, instead, is to provide the maximum amount of goods for those who have money, whether they live in the U.S.A., Europe, Brazil, Guatemala, or elsewhere. The affluent have enormous power to divert resources away from where they are most needed to where they can be most profitable.

The hungry are victims of what might be called "video-game economics." The "video-game theory of economic development" goes something like this. It is profitable to produce and sell nonessential goods such as video games. If enough profit can be made by producing and selling nonessential goods, sizeable investments will be made in this area. This will create jobs. Production of nonessential goods will eventually create enough jobs so that everyone will have sufficient income to buy the basic necessities of life and other things as well.

"Video-game economics" overlooks several problems. First, producing video games and other nonessential goods wastes enormous quantities of resources. Secondly, investment in video games precludes investment in other areas more central to meeting minimal living standards. Thirdly, the able-bodied could have jobs and produce essential goods rather than video games. Finally, many workers who produce nonessential goods are part of a "cheap labor supply." They are employed but they do not earn sufficient income to provide for their families adequately.

The tragedy of most U.S. corporate investment and the foreign policy necessary to protect that investment is that it unites the rich worldwide in a common struggle for the use of resources that preempts their use by the poor to meet basic needs. The international economy is based on unhealthy alliances that foster maldevelopment: wasteful production and overconsumption for some; underconsumption of basic goods for others. The death of compassion is reflected in personal and institutional priorities that favor luxury wants over human needs. Hundreds of thousands are literally starving to death in a sea of unhealthy, wasteful affluence.

DEHUMANIZING THE POOR

It is easier to tolerate the starvation, torture, or murder of others if we can distance ourselves from them. When we apply a dehumanizing label to individuals and groups, we diminish any claim they might have on our humanity. Jesus encouraged the lawyer in the compassionate Samaritan parable to break out of the prison of bias and hardheartedness. This was possible only if the lawyer could relate to the Samaritan as a neighbor. Jesus encourages us to read the parable today and see the hungry as our neighbors. Unfortunately, the poor are for us more often statistics than living, breathing persons. The individual and collective agony of hunger is silenced by dehumanizing labels such as "migrant worker," "vagrant," "subversive," "communist," or "Marxist-Leninist."

I visited Honduras several times in 1983 and 1984. Honduras was deeply involved in U.S. efforts to destabilize Nicaragua and I was interested in the effect of such efforts on Honduran society. It became clear in meetings with labor leaders, church groups, and officials from the Honduran Human Rights Commission that the situation was dramatically deteriorating as a result of U.S. involvement.[29] The group I traveled with had materials confiscated by the Honduran security forces and we were harassed by a member of a Honduran death squad. We questioned the president of the Honduran Assembly about our treatment and the reports of human rights violations we had heard of. He told us there were "no human rights violations in Honduras. Besides," he added, "communists have no rights."

The problem is that behind the "communist" label there are real human beings who are being harassed, tortured, killed. Nearly everyone who works with the poor or seeks social change is labeled a communist. In addition, communists are people whose ideas and basic human rights should be respected.

In Honduras I met an old friend who is an executive with the United Methodist Church in New York City. He told me a story about his recent visit to Guatemala, a story that illustrates the need to see the faces of neighbors behind the communist label.

The best land in Guatemala is owned by a small minority. Many Guatemalans must farm land with steep, highly erodable, slopes. The Methodist Church funded a project in Guatemala to reduce erosion through terracing. The project was successful. Many of the villagers became self-sufficient in food and no longer had to migrate for several months of the year as seasonal workers on coffee and cotton plantations. A project such as this is considered communistic and subversive in Guatemala. The plantation owners were worried that the idea might spread to other villages and reduce their exploitable labor supply. Death squads, in conjunction with the Guatemalan army, were sent in and the project was destroyed.

Bishop Lawrence H. Welsh in a pastoral letter on Guatemala reminds us that the Amerindians there (a majority of the population) and hungry persons everywhere are our brothers and sisters:

> I believe it to be very important for you . . . to know that the Indian people . . . in Guatemala are very much our brothers and sisters in Christ and their suffering and persecution is indeed our own. We are, in Christ, one family, and the hunger, harassment, torture, or unjust death of one member of this family is a pain felt by all.[30]

FIVE CONCLUSIONS

The biblical logic of the majorities, with its emphasis on the well-being of the poor, equity, and sufficiency for all, contrasts sharply with the reality of international and national economies responsible for human suffering as the cost of maintaining the privilege of the rich. Using the biblical logic of the majorities as the basis for a critique, it is possible to draw the following conclusions:

First, *concentration of land and other wealth-producing resources contributes to economic and spiritual decay.* Economic and spiritual health in and outside Central America depend on breaking the cycle of indebtedness and on a redistribution of wealth, land, and power.

Secondly, *the economy of the U.S.A. and the international economy as a whole fail miserably when judged in relation to domestic and world hunger and poverty.* The logic of capitalism clearly collides with the biblical logic of the majorities. The production, availability, and consumption of luxuries does not redeem economies that tolerate or even encourage the exploitation of the poor. These economies are a major impediment to economic and spiritual health worldwide.

Thirdly, *"value-free" economics is an illusion.* "Value-free" economics reinforces the values and interests of the rich and powerful at the expense of the poor. "Value-free" economics clashes with *the biblical bias in favor of the poor,* in favor of priorities and policies that promote sufficiency for all as central to both economic and spiritual health. Christians are only some of the many participants who shape economic systems and priorities. It is important that we seek to be a leaven that works for fundamental changes in the U.S. and world economy. Christians committed to the biblical logic of the majorities should work for a dramatic redistribution of wealth and wealth-producing resources, agrarian reform, debt relief, conservation, fairer terms of trade, public participation or control of key areas of production and banking, and the targeting of industry and agriculture to meet basic human needs.

Fourthly, although this chapter has focused primarily on injustices in the world economy and within underdeveloped countries, *the biblical logic of the majorities can serve as a guideline by which to examine domestic economic priorities*. For example, the economic programs enacted by the Reagan administration since 1980 have inflicted major hardship on the poor. These programs involved massive tax cuts for the rich, large cutbacks in social services, and huge military spending increases. The top 3 percent of households received 17 percent of the tax cuts; the bottom 22 percent received 3 percent of the tax cuts. The latter group lost more in benefit reductions than it gained in tax breaks. For example, the cumulative effect of tax breaks and budget cuts on households with incomes of less than $10,000 was an average *loss* of $260. Households with incomes of more than $80,000 *gained* an average of $19,190.[31] Policies such as these are totally incompatible with the biblical guidelines of justice, equality, and sufficiency.

Finally, the logic of the majorities leads me to conclude that *the values, assumptions, and workings of the capitalist system are so hostile to biblical values that capitalism must be judged a fatally flawed system*.

Adam Smith, the first economic architect of capitalism, insisted that the best economy is one that enables individuals to maximize their private greed. This, he argued, would result in the public good. It is hard to imagine a premise more distant from biblical roots and values. Imagine the rich young man coming to Jesus (Mark 10:17ff.) to ask about eternal life. Jesus looks at the young man, loves him, and says: "There is one more thing you need to do. Go and maximize your private greed because it will result in the public good."

A condemnation of capitalism does not imply that all economic incentives are unjust or that all socialist systems are inherently just. However, it does seem that the values of Christianity converge much more closely with those of socialism. The fact that Christians in the U.S.A. have a morbid fear of socialism is related to an idolatrous commitment to capitalism and to a false identification of all socialist options with those of the Soviet Union.

Capitalism concentrates wealth and power; the biblical writers seek to redistribute it. Capitalism spurns equity and targets production to the profit-desires and the demands of the wealthy; the biblical writers look directly to the needs of the poor. Capitalism measures success by gross national product; the biblical writers look to the social well-being of the poor. Capitalism stresses ownership; the biblical writers stress stewardship. Capitalism thrives on greed; the biblical writers condemn greed and selfishness, and call us to service, sharing, and compassion. Capitalism promotes unlimited possession and consumption as a means to ultimate fulfillment; the biblical writers stress sufficiency, the importance of setting limits, and wealth as a roadblock to authentic spirituality.

The toll that hunger takes on individuals and families is profoundly personal. A series of socially induced personal tragedies builds into a collective agony called world hunger. It is this personal and collective agony that compels us to examine the personal and social obstacles to compassion. Individual compassionate acts can be blocked or undone by social systems that concentrate landholdings, encourage alliances between elites, foster and exploit indebtedness, and muddle reality through dehumanizing labels. It is not enough to offer starving children a meal while knowingly or unknowingly supporting economic policies that are responsible for their hunger. What is required is a politics of compassion that embodies personal and social commitments to build justice into economic relationships, lifestyles, political systems, and governmental policies. Christians must be freed from the idolatry of capitalism if they are to be a spiritually whole people working for socio-economic justice.

Chapter 4

Central America:
A Call to Conversion

You come here speaking of Latin America, but this is not important. Nothing important can come from the South. History has never been produced in the South. The axis of history starts in Moscow, goes to Bonn, crosses over to Washington, and then goes to Tokyo. What happens in the South is of no importance.

Henry Kissinger to Gabriel Valdes,
Foreign Minister of Chile, June 1969

But God chose what is foolish in the world to shame the wise, God chose what is weak in the world to shame the strong, God chose what is low and despised in the world . . . to bring to nothing things that are, so that no human being might boast in the presence of God.

1 Corinthians 1:27-29

The crisis in Central America looks very different when viewed from the vantage point of power and privilege or from that of poverty and oppression. The biblical writers insist that although we all have eyes and ears, it is the perspective of the poor that transmits sight and sound with clarity. The logic of the majorities today in Central America is in violent conflict with the privileges of the rich, including the full weight of power from the wealthiest country in the world. We are witnessing a historical reenactment of the biblical drama in which the rich are confronted with the choice of serving wealth or God, of selling all and following Jesus or clinging to power and privilege. The task for Christians in the U.S.A. is to remove our ideological blinkers and free the

57

nation from the economic determinism that insists on the pursuit of narrow economic interests as the fundamental goal of U.S. foreign policy.

Salvation, in the biblical sense of healing and reconciliation, is still possible. Hundreds of thousands of lives, which could be lost in the event of a regional war, *can* be saved, millions of others *can* be rescued from malnutrition and despair, and the American public *can* effectively alter the course of its national history, which at the present time moves steadily toward disaster. It is both ironic and paradoxical that one of the principal focuses of world attention today is the tiny country of El Salvador—the land of the Savior.

The purpose of this chapter is to assess the impact of U.S. foreign policy in Central America in light of the biblical logic of the majorities. The economic and ideological roots of present U.S. policy and their relationship to the suffering of the poor will receive particular emphasis. Attention will also be given to specific ways in which redemptive challenges are being posed in the concrete struggles of Central American peoples. The aspirations of the poor are challenging the arrogance of power, demanding a new social order, and offering practical historical examples of economic alternatives more in tune with the biblical logic of the majorities.

THE SETTING

Nicaragua is in the midst of profound changes. The Sandinistas, who took power with the ouster of Anastasio Somoza in 1979 and who received a strong mandate from the Nicaraguan people in the elections of November 1984, are the most independent-minded leaders in the region. They are committed to such principles as a mixed economy, nonalignment with major world power blocs, and political pluralism within the framework of a socio-economic revolutionary program designed to improve the lives of the long-exploited poor.

The U.S.A. has labeled Nicaragua "totalitarian" while itself engaging in numerous illegal actions including the mining of Nicaraguan ports by the CIA, repeated violation of Nicaraguan airspace by U.S. spy planes, and the production and distribution of a manual that encouraged assassination of key Nicaraguan officials. Nicaragua daily experiences attacks from U.S.-backed counter-revolutionary groups (contras) operating from bases in Honduras and Costa Rica. The U.S.A. also carried out a sophisticated effort to disrupt and discredit the Nicaraguan elections. The intense economic, military, and diplomatic pressures are aimed at the clear yet diplomatically inadmissible goal of ousting the Sandinistas. President Reagan has stated that the only way he would tolerate the Sandinistas would be "if they say uncle." He has described the contras, who killed nearly eight thousand Nicaraguans in the first five years after the ouster of Somoza, as "the moral equivalent of the founding fathers of the United States." Despite a congressional study identifying 46 of the top 48 contra military leaders as former Somoza national guardsmen and numerous human rights reports documenting contra atrocities, the

U.S. Congress approved $27 million in contra aid in June 1985.

The most likely future prospects for Nicaragua include a continuation and escalation of the U.S.-sponsored "low-intensity war" (with terroristic attacks on outlying villages, health centers, and key economic targets without a significant number of *U.S.* casualties), a U.S.-backed regional war using surrogate troops from neighboring countries, or a full-scale U.S. invasion.

El Salvador is in the midst of a prolonged civil war. The March 1984 electoral victory of José Napoleón Duarte provided cover for the U.S. goal of a military victory. The Salvadoran government continues to be shaky, dependent on the military, and powerless to alter the underlying economic structures that have been the source of social unrest for generations. Duarte's strategy is to give the appearance that he and the country are moving to the political center, whereas the reality is that the country remains firmly in the grasp of a powerful right wing.

Differences between appearance and reality will probably continue. Duarte met with rebel leaders in May 1984. The U.S.A. at the same time increased military assistance to El Salvador by 140 percent. This steep rise in military assistance enhanced both the political power of the military and its ability to escalate the war. U.S. aid has led to an increase in the number of Huey helicopters from eighteen to forty-nine. These helicopters, along with heavily armed gunships, allow the military to carry out airmobile tactics developed in Vietnam.

The appearance rather than substance of strategies for peace also serves to deceive the people of El Salvador. Salvadorans want peace and the vast majority of them either support the rebels or understand that the rebels must be included in any negotiated settlement. Duarte's appearance of openness raises their expectations and hopes for peace, but his actions strengthen the hand of the conservative military, the principal obstacle to peace. All this could lead to another wave of violence in El Salvador. If the U.S.-backed government continues to falter, U.S. troops could be sent in.

Honduras is the second poorest country in the hemisphere (only Haiti is poorer). It has become the key military agent in carrying out U.S. foreign policy objectives in Central America, particularly the destabilization of Nicaragua. Major military exercises involving U.S. and Honduran troops have been carried out every year since 1983. U.S. troops are scheduled to remain in Honduras at least through 1987. Despite civilian elections, which began in 1981, the power in Honduras clearly resides with the Honduran military and the U.S. embassy. U.S. efforts to use Honduras as a military base from which to destabilize Nicaragua were orchestrated in their initial phases by John Negroponte, then U.S. ambassador, seasoned in Vietnam.

U.S. efforts to militarize Honduras have largely been successful—eight airbases have been constructed or improved, maneuvers to intimidate Nicaragua have been carried out, support for the contras has been facilitated, and a regional training base has been established at Puerto Castilla. However, these "successes" have been marred by notable contradictions that complicate U.S.

policy: U.S. support for a corrupt general led to a shake-up in the Honduran military that strengthened the position of nationalistic officers; the influx of U.S. military assistance has been accompanied by increased human rights violations including death and disappearances at the hands of death squads; Nicaraguan contra tactics of rape, pillage, and murder have spilled over into Honduras, fueling resentments and fears; the failure to resolve a long-standing border dispute between Honduras and El Salvador (the cause of a war in 1969) resulted in the refusal of the Hondurans to train Salvadoran soldiers at Puerto Castilla. Many Hondurans are beginning to realize that if they go to war in Central America it would probably not be with land-rich Nicaragua, which supports regional efforts for disarmament, but with land-hungry El Salvador, which with U.S. support is becoming the most potent military force in the region.

The use of Honduras to meet U.S. foreign policy goals is dividing Honduran society and creating the conditions in which social rebellion is likely. U.S. efforts to destabilize Nicaragua and win a military victory in El Salvador could easily result in the destabilization of Honduras.

Costa Rica has a long history of democratic institutions and social stability. More equitable land tenure systems and social programs have until recently set Costa Rica apart from the turmoil of its neighbors. The problem is that Costa Rica is nearly bankrupt and therefore susceptible to economic pressures. The U.S.A is using such pressures to push Costa Rica into regional efforts to overthrow the Nicaraguan government. Diplomatically, Costa Rica is at the center of a propaganda war against the Sandinistas. Militarily, it allows its territory to be used as a base by a Nicaraguan counterinsurgency group seeking the downfall of the Nicaraguan government. Without an army since 1946, Costa Rica is now allowing U.S. military advisors to train Costa Rican counterinsurgency battalions.

Once again the U.S. government is walking a thin line. Some civilian leaders in Costa Rica look at their Latin American neighbors and see that militarization often reduces or eliminates civilian power. They are not eager to comply with U.S. desires to militarize their country. However, it is also true that the militarization of Costa Rica has internal supporters. The rationalization given for such support is fear about a possible invasion from Nicaragua, but it seems more likely that the real concern is that some of the estimated 70 percent of the Costa Rican population living below the official poverty line may grow restless in the worsening economic situation. The overriding reality is that Costa Rica will collapse without U.S. support. Tensions within this dynamic of dependency will undoubtedly sharpen with the passage of time.

Guatemala is less in the news but the economic stakes of U.S. companies are greatest there. Coups within the military brought new tyrants to power in 1982 and 1983. Political repression, torture, and hunger are institutionalized realities of Guatemalan life. Guatemala is a powder keg waiting to explode. The U.S.A. first circumvented then lifted restrictions on military aid, increased economic assistance, and set the stage for greater military involvement. However, a U.S.-approved coup in the summer of 1983, which ousted a born-again Christian, Rios Montt, and brought into power General Oscar Humberto Mejía Víctores, has done little to overcome Guatemalan reluctance to participate in any major way in regional efforts to destabilize Nicaragua.

Political changes in Central America are difficult to predict. U.S. troops could become involved in a war in El Salvador or in a prolonged regional war. Guatemala could explode, prompting a much larger commitment of U.S. weapons and troops. Honduras and Nicaragua could go to war because of Honduran complicity in the U.S. contra war. The U.S.A. could send marines to Nicaragua as it has so often in this century, or it could invade Nicaragua using proxy troops from Central American countries. It is even possible that regional peace efforts such as that of the Contadora nations—Panama, Venezuela, Colombia, and Mexico— could succeed in reducing tensions and open up the possibility for regional economic development.

The U.S.A. will be a major participant in determining the course of events in Central America. It is important, therefore, that both the logic and likely consequences of U.S. foreign policy be examined. Four commonsense observations from the previous chapter should be kept in mind as discussion continues on U.S. foreign policy and the logic of the majorities: powerful persons and groups make money doing things that cause hunger; providing guns to these powerful groups reinforces their power and perpetuates hunger; dehumanizing labels are used to distract attention from other issues; no one likes being hungry or oppressed.

PROTECTING ECONOMIC INTERESTS

The primary purpose of U.S. foreign policy is to insure that the international economy, and the policies of individual nations within it, serve U.S. corporate interests. A CBS documentary describes how a democratically elected government in Guatemala commits itself to land reform and offends the United Fruit Company. The U.S. response is to train Guatemalan insurgents and U.S. mercenaries in nearby Honduras, launch a CIA-backed invasion, and install a government favorable to U.S. business interests. United Fruit had friends in high places. At the time of the U.S. intervention, John Foster Dulles, a longtime legal advisor to the company, was U.S. secretary of state; his brother Allen Dulles was director of the CIA; Henry Cabot Lodge, a large stockholder and member of the United Fruit Company board of directors, was the U.S. ambassador to the United Nations; John Moors Cabot, a large shareholder, was assistant secretary of state for inter-American affairs; and Walter Bedell Smith, a predecessor of Allen Dulles as director of the CIA, became president of the United Fruit Company after the overthrow of the Arbenz government.

This example is graphic but not exceptional. The United States has consistently brought significant power to bear in defense of economic interests that victimize the hungry. U.S. intervention takes a variety of forms:

• *A commitment of U.S. troops*—Panama, 1908, 1912, and 1918; Cuba, 1906–09, 1912, 1917–23; Nicaragua, 1912–25, 1926–33; Dominican Republic, 1916–24, 1965; Haiti, 1914–35; Vietnam, 1958–73; Grenada, 1983–84; Lebanon, 1983–84.

• *CIA covert activities,* including the ouster of democratically elected governments in Guatemala, 1954, and Chile, 1973; the Bay of Pigs operation against Castro in Cuba, 1961; efforts to destabilize the Michael Manley government in Jamaica in the mid-1970s; and efforts to destabilize the government of Nicaragua.

• *Economic warfare,* including blockades (Cuba and Vietnam), restrictions on food aid (India, Chile, and Nicaragua), and efforts to block international loans (Chile, Jamaica, and Nicaragua).

• *Routine military assistance and sales to repressive governments,* including South Korea, the Philippines, El Salvador, and most of the underdeveloped countries with whom we are aligned.

The use of U.S. military power to protect economic interests is clear in the case of Central America but should not be overstated. U.S. business involvement in the region is relatively modest. It takes three principal forms: direct investment, bank loans, and export-import trade. The figures below testify to the modest nature of U.S. business involvement in Central America, at least in relation to all foreign operations. However, collectively these figures translate into a significant economic impact on the region:

• More than 1,400 businesses in Central America have some U.S. ownership.

• Seventy of the 100 largest U.S. corporations conduct operations there.

• The U.S. Department of Commerce estimates that direct investments of U.S. financial and industrial companies in Central America had a book value of $4.8 billion in 1980. This was based on an accounting of direct investments in excess of $500,000.

• U.S. transnational banks had $3.3 billion in outstanding loans to the private and public sector in Central America in 1981.

• The U.S. Department of Commerce estimates that for every dollar that U.S. companies invest in Latin America, three dollars accrue to investors. Returns are higher in Central America.

• Central America represents a $2.6 billion market for U.S. goods each year. The U.S.A. imports $1.1 billion worth of goods annually, including 69 percent of its bananas, 15 percent of its coffee, 14 percent of total beef imports, and 17 percent of its sugar. In 1980, the Central American trade deficit with the U.S.A. was $2.6 billion.[32]

With these statistics alone, one would be hard pressed to explain the dramatic militarization of Central America by the U.S.A. It is true that U.S. economic investments have aggravated inequalities and social tensions in the region, and that the U.S.A. has responded to these social tensions with military power rather than with economic accommodation to the needs of the majorities. However, present levels of military investment seem to defy even a

Pentagon- or business-based assessment of relative costs and benefits. The militarization of Central America must be understood in the broader context of fears about strategic and economic interests:

> U.S. interests in the nations of Central America and the Caribbean are considerable and, as is often the case, form an inseparable blur of business and military-strategic concerns. The primary business concerns are in oil and shipping. Nearly half of U.S. imported goods pass through the Panama Canal or the Gulf of Mexico, including two-thirds of our imported oil. In addition, 56 percent of the refined oil imported to the U.S. comes from refineries in the Caribbean islands, the oil companies having been lured there by deep-water ports, cheap labor, and the absence of environmental regulations. Enormous and attractive oil reserves lie in Mexico, Venezuela, and Trinidad, with the probability of similar untapped oil supplies in other countries, particularly Guatemala. The region also supplies almost all U.S. bauxite, the ore used to make aluminum, and it has sizable investments from U.S. agribusiness corporations.[33]

Progressive governments in Central America and the Caribbean would undoubtedly alter present economic relationships with the United States. However, it seems to be the assumption of U.S. policy-makers that progressive governments would automatically refuse to sell oil or other goods to the U.S.A. or that they would take steps to block international shipping. The choices seem to be narrowed to domination *by* the U.S.A. or economic strangulation *of* the U.S.A. The fact that there are other options, including relationships involving mutual respect, is not seriously considered by U.S. policy-makers. At any rate, the convergence of the desire to protect both narrow and broader economic interests has resulted in the militarization of Central America. The dramatic increase in U.S. military involvement in the recent past is illustrated by the following figures:

• From 1950 to 1970 the U.S.A. spent an average of $7.5 million per year to equip and train Central American military. In 1980, U.S. military aid increased to $8.8 million; in 1981 to $44.8 million; and in 1982 to $199.1 million. U.S. military assistance to El Salvador alone exceeded $196.5 million in 1984.

• From 1962 to 1982 the U.S.A. spent more than $42 million in training at least 22,500 soldiers and officers from Central America—not including 1,600 Salvadoran troops trained in 1982 with emergency funds from the Department of Defense.

• The U.S. government provides direct grants of military aid through the Military Assistance Program (MAP). More than $141 million in MAP grants poured into Central America from 1950 to 1982—70 percent of it granted in 1981 and 1982. The U.S.A. also provides indirect grants for military purposes through the Economic Support Fund (ESF) created under the Foreign Assistance Act. ESF aid can be given under "special economic, political, or security conditions." Representative Clarence Long offers this assessment of the purpose of ESF aid: "You know that economic supporting assistance is simply a device to say to a country, 'Look, take your money and buy weapons, and we will cover your exchange problems with it.' "[34]

• Throughout much of 1983 and 1984 the Pentagon encircled Nicaragua with the longest "war games" in U.S. history, involving up to 34,000 troops along with naval forces with fire power greater than that employed during the Vietnam war.[35]

• In January 1984, a national bipartisan commission on Central America, widely referred to as the Kissinger Commission, issued a report on U.S. policy in Central America. The report recommended greatly increased military assistance to the region. For example, the Kissinger Commission states that "the present level of U.S. military assistance to El Salvador is far too low. . . ." Although the commission did not recommend a precise dollar figure, it indicated "that the U.S. Department of Defense estimates that it would take approximately $400 million in U.S. military assistance in 1984 and 1985 to break the military stalemate."[36] *Military assistance to El Salvador alone would mark a 4,500 percent increase over levels of military assistance to all of Central America in 1980, a 400 percent increase over 1982 levels.*

IGNORING THE LOGIC OF THE MAJORITIES

The economic roots of social crisis in Central America are relatively easy to identify. Little or no attention has been paid to the biblical guidelines of sufficiency, equity, and the well-being of the poor as keys to economic and spiritual health. The logic of capital has clearly dominated the patterns of landownership and use to the detriment of the poor. The same is true in the areas of manufacturing and trade. This can be illustrated by a brief examination of recent regional economic history.

The problem of regional development in Central America is highlighted in its point of departure. The single most important event that has shaped the recent political and economic history of Central America was the overthrow of the U.S.-backed dictatorship of Fulgencio Batista in Cuba in 1959. U.S interest in economic development in Central America and elsewhere was rooted in the fear of other Cubas. From the perspective of the U.S.A., development in Central America and elsewhere was not seen as a *process of liberation,* wherein an oppressed people demands and receives sufficient power to implement decisions based on a logic of the majorities. On the contrary, economic development was viewed as *a means of counterinsurgency to be planned and implemented from above through the imposition of the logic of capital.* It is not necessary to be cynical or impute malicious intent to the architects of the logic of capital. It is quite likely that they believe, and continue to believe, the following assumptions:

• What is good for capital and for U.S. business will be good for the receiving nation and its people.

• Development guided by the logic of capital benefits the poor majority enough to diffuse social tensions and block aspirations for more fundamental changes that would lead to economic priorities more in tune with the logic of the majorities.

• Economic development efforts need to be supplemented by military assistance programs to insure that social change be kept within limits defined by the United States.

The U.S. response to the overthrow of Batista in Cuba was the Alliance for Progress, which coupled developmental assistance with counterinsurgency training, and the formation of the Central American Common Market (CACM). The U.S. government lobbied hard to substitute the CACM for a regional effort already under discussion within the United Nations. The UN plan was geared more directly to the needs of the region and to the logic of the majorities. It intended to link up the Central American countries into a larger economic unit in order to create economies that could provide sufficient markets to justify regional industrialization efforts. The emphasis was on balanced industrialization, maximum use of local resources, and development of indigenous industries. The UN plan stressed the need for centralized planning and strong governmental participation in order to avoid duplication. It also advocated constructive use of tariffs to avoid setbacks from international competition.

The U.S.A., firmly enveloped by the logic of capital, objected to the anti-free market nature of the UN plan. It offered $100 million for the starting of the CACM, which was enough to sway Central American elites. The results of the CACM were at odds with the intentions of the UN plan. The logic of capital smothered the aspects of the UN program that might have served the interests of the majorities. For example, the CACM resulted in increased investments by and profits for foreign firms rather than the mobilization of local and regional capital, extensive loss of local control of existent industries bought out by foreign multinationals, and a further integration into the world economy without regional integration and development. Production encouraged by the CACM was by and for elites, and economic growth was steady but unbalanced, with few jobs created and problems of income-distribution aggravated. The failure of the logic of capital to meet the basic needs of the poor and its propensity to aggravate inequalities explain social turmoil that has been met by a furious U.S. military response.

Victims of Ignorance and Malice

U.S. foreign policy in Central America and beyond has tragic consequences for poor majorities. They are victimized by policies that are shortsighted or based on mistaken assumptions. Some U.S. policy-makers are bound by the narrow perspective of Fred Sherwood. Hunger and poverty lie outside their worldview. There is the good life on the one hand, and that which threatens it on the other. Keith Parker, manager for Bank of America operations in

Guatemala, states with stark simplicity the implications of this worldview for those who work for social change in oppressive societies:

> What they [the Guatemalan government] should do is declare martial law. There you catch somebody; they go to a military court. The colonels are sitting there; you're guilty, you're shot. It works very well.[37]

Such a procedure has been more or less routine in Guatemala since the 1954 coup that ousted Jacobo Arbenz. Between 1966 and 1976 the U.S.A. supported a series of military governments that, according to Amnesty International, were directly linked to paramilitary death squads responsible for the murder of twenty-two thousand Guatemalans. This terror was carried out in part by some of the thirty-two thousand Guatemalan police trained through the U.S. Office of Public Safety.[38]

The Kissinger Commission report recommends that "military aid and military sales should be authorized if Guatemala meets . . . human rights conditions" (p. 104). This could open the door for a massive increase in U.S. military assistance to Guatemala. If El Salvador is a guide, we can expect that human rights violations will not be an obstacle to receiving aid.

Amnesty International, the Nobel Peace Prize–winning human rights group based in London, released a report in May of 1984 that accused the U.S.-backed government in El Salvador of ordering the deaths of many of the estimated forty thousand persons murdered there in the previous five years. The report charged that it is the "authorities themselves who lie behind the wholesale extrajudicial executions."[39] Despite this report, both the Reagan administration and Congress seized upon the March 1984 election of Duarte to increase U.S. military assistance to $196.5 million. The foreign aid authorization bill for fiscal year 1985, which authorized military aid for El Salvador, did so *without regard to progress in upholding human rights.* This is particularly ironic in light of the fact that one of the worst periods of human rights abuses in the history of El Salvador was from 1980 to 1982, a period that included the provisional presidency of Duarte! Not surprisingly, in May 1984, the Inter-American Commission on Human Rights of the Organization of American States issued a report asserting that the Salvadoran human rights record had improved little during the presidency of Duarte.[40]

The Reagan administration is clearly not interested in letting human rights issues stand in the way of its pursuit of military solutions to the problems of Central America. Henry Kissinger and several other prominent members of the bipartisan Kissinger Commission were ardently opposed to any linkage between human rights and U.S. military assistance to the region.[41] Congress is also balking on previous human rights commitments.

In 1977 Congress passed legislation banning military assistance to gross human rights violators, including Guatemala. Military shipments continued despite the ban. In 1980 the Reagan administration bypassed Congress and sent military equipment to Guatemala. It did so by reclassifying jeeps and trucks as nonmilitary. The State Department formally lifted the military embargo against Guatemala in January 1983 and approved the sale of helicopter spare parts. Human rights groups report that these helicopters were used to massacre several thousand Guatemalan Amerindians. For fiscal year 1985 Guatemala is slated to receive $52.5 million in economic aid from the U.S.A. including $12.5 million in economic support funds that can be used for military purposes.[42] Trends such as these thrill Fred Sherwood but it takes little imagination to assess their likely impact on the poor. Sherwood's logic is simple and straightforward:

> Why should we be worried about the death squads? They're bumping off the commies, our enemies. I'd give them more power. Hell, I'd get some cartridges if I could. . . . Why should we criticize them? The death squads—I'm for it. . . . We all feel that he [President Reagan] is our savior.[43]

There is one other means to ensure that weapons get to countries that are economically important to the U.S.A. yet subject to restrictions because of a poor human rights record: the use of a third country supplier. Israel, which receives nearly $7 million daily in U.S. aid, is a major weapons supplier to El Salvador, Guatemala, Honduras, and South Africa. Congress was upset in the spring of 1984 when it was revealed that the CIA had helped mine Nicaraguan harbors and carry out raids against Nicaraguan ports. It was widely feared that if Congress were to cut off direct funding for the counterrevolutionaries seeking to overthrow the Nicaraguan government, the Reagan administration would turn to Israel. In a *Minneapolis Tribune* article entitled "Aid to Contras Can Continue without Congress," political scientist William Leo Grande wrote:

> Israel is a prime candidate. The Likud government has already positioned Israel as a major arms supplier to rightist regimes in Latin America; to become the contras' patron could be seen as a logical next step. No item in the foreign assistance budget has greater support, particularly among Democrats, than aid to Israel, thus making the Israeli option virtually immune to congressional retribution [April 24, 1984].

The result of the third party option is bloody repression with the appearance of unbloodied hands.

The Kissinger Commission

The report of the Kissinger Commission for the most part moves past the maliciousness of Keith Parker and Fred Sherwood to misunderstanding. Whereas Fred Sherwood and his allies ignore the problem of hunger, the commission acknowledges that hunger and poverty are fertile ground for social turmoil. However, the Kissinger Commission fails to connect hunger and social turmoil to the logic of capital associated with U.S. economic investments. Therefore, it calls for economic assistance between 1985 and 1989 totaling $8 billion. This aid, according to the commission report, should be contingent upon Central American pursuit of economic policies that "encourage private enterprise" and "create favorable investment climates" (p. 54). Moreover, the glimpses of creative analysis about the relationship between poverty and social turmoil that one finds in the report are obscured by an overwhelming preoccupation with military solutions in the region.

There is ample historical evidence to suggest that the result of a massive increase in economic aid and investment, coupled with the pursuit of military solutions, will be disaster for poor majorities. The results are likely to be more hunger, greater inequality, and increased social turmoil. John Booth, a political science professor at the University of Texas at San Antonio has written an excellent paper on the socio-economic and political roots of rebellion in Central America. Booth, who has extensive Central American experience, wondered why Nicaragua (under Somoza), El Salvador, and Guatemala exploded into civil wars, whereas Honduras and Costa Rica did not. He concludes:

• "Differences in the rate and nature of economic growth, income, and wealth distribution, and governmental response to mobilization, account for the occurrence of insurrections in Nicaragua (under Somoza), El Salvador, and Guatemala, and for the lack of rebellions in Honduras and Costa Rica."

• The countries that erupted into widespread violence were those that participated most fully in the Alliance for Progress, an aid program similar in many respects to the recommendations of the Kissinger Commission. Booth attributes the connection between participation in the Alliance for Progress and widespread violence to the fact that industrial development promoted by the alliance and the Central American Common Market (CACM) "sharply increased economic inequality in some nations by accelerating the shifts of wealth and income away from working-class groups."

• In each of the Central American countries there were social conditions, such as poverty and hunger, that could lead to unrest. The key ingredient for determining levels of social unrest was how governments responded to the demands of groups working for change. "Central American governments responded differently . . . those of Nicaragua [under Somoza], El Salvador, and Guatemala implemented severe political repression in order to silence demands, while in Costa Rica and Honduras . . . response to unrest and to new citizen demands was comparatively moderate."

• "External intervention does not constitute a major cause of rebellions in Central America . . . they stem from powerful domestic socio-psychological forces unleashed by social change and by the behavior of regimes."[44]

If John Booth's analysis is correct, and all my experiences in Central America confirm his views, then the Kissinger Commission is dead wrong. The commission makes three fundamental errors. First, it fails to see that U.S.

economic investment can be a problem. The Kissinger Commission stresses U.S. *neglect* of Central America and calls for a five-year aid commitment of $8 billion. Unfortunately, the problem of U.S. policy in Central America is not neglect but *exploitation*. The U.S.A. has actively intervened into the affairs of this region both militarily and economically for nearly a century. The result of this active intervention is hunger, poverty, and social unrest throughout the region. It is not that $8 billion could not be used to relieve poverty in Central America, but that it will not be used effectively given present assumptions and priorities.

Secondly, the dramatic increase in military assistance to the region will be used to put down political protest and dissent. It will do so precisely at a time when economic investments will further aggravate inequalities. The results will likely be increased hunger, poverty, political repression, and social turmoil.

Thirdly, the Kissinger Commission is obsessed with an East-West interpretation of Central American reality. In the eyes of the commission, poverty is common to the region and yet poverty alone cannot explain revolution. Therefore, it must be outside communist infiltration that moves a populace from poverty to rebellion. Sooner or later the commission traces all rebellion to the doorsteps of Cuba and the Soviet Union. This focus on outside communist provocation allows the commission to ignore the fact that a people can be moved from poverty to rebellion by economic inequalities aggravated by U.S. aid and investment, and by political repression carried out with U.S. money and weaponry. The obsession with outside communist infiltration ensures that commission recommendations, if followed, will repeat past failures. Referring to the opposition movement in El Salvador, former U.S. Ambassador Robert White said:

> The heart of the problem grew out of intolerable poverty and constant terror; it is authentic and homegrown. Our policy-makers refuse to recognize this fact; that is why their policies don't work.[45]

If implemented, the Kissinger Commission recommendations will fail because they are based on the same faulty assumptions as the Alliance for Progress. The goals of both ignore the logic of the majorities. They are predicated on the notion that development is essential if social unrest, a threat to U.S. corporate interests, is to be averted. The hope is that the U.S. government can promote and protect U.S. corporate interests and at the same time modernize and reform the economies and governments of underdeveloped countries. The problem is that the protection of U.S. corporate interests generally clashes with goals for authentic reforms that are desperately needed to break the cycle of hunger and poverty. When this conflict becomes clear, idealistic goals give way to pragmatism: a military solution in defense of U.S. corporate interests. If we fail to learn these lessons, we may have to be reminded of the assessment made by Edward Kennedy in 1970 when he graphically portrayed the failure of the Alliance for Progress:

Economic growth per capita [in Latin America] is less than before the Alliance for Progress began; in the previous eight years U.S. business has repatriated $8.3 billion in private profits, more than three times the total of new investment; the land remains in the hands of a few; one-third of the rural labor force is unemployed and *thirteen constitutional governments have been overthrown since the Alliance was launched.*[46]

Hunger and Ideology

A significant cause of world hunger and a major impediment to compassion is the ideology that undergirds U.S. foreign policy. U.S. foreign policy is based on two fundamental assumptions. First, *the U.S.A. has the power and the moral authority to manage change within other countries.* One U.S. senator told me that "the U.S. has the moral authority to do what it wants to in Central America because we're right." The Kissinger Commission report states that the U.S.A. is involved in Central America is order to "preserve the moral authority of the United States. To be perceived by others as a nation that does what is right *because* it is right is one of this country's principal assets" (p. 37). Other political officials, both Republicans and Democrats insist that "we can't lose El Salvador," or "we can't lose Central America," as though they belong to us. Their attitudes are similar to those of Undersecretary of State Robert Olds in 1927:

We do control the destinies of Central America and we do so for the simple reason that the national interest absolutely dictates such a course. . . . Until now Central America has always understood that governments which we recognize and support stay in power, while those we do not recognize and support fail.[47]

It is a characteristic of empires to assign moral authority to imperial ambitions. Moral authority must always be linked with rightful certitude. Unfortunately, powerful countries are often arrogant, blind, and wrong. This is as true of the United States as it is of the Soviet Union. Neither Afghanistan nor El Salvador is a showcase of moral or ethical foreign policies.

Arrogance is blinding in many ways. For example, one need not be an expert to know that if the U.S.A. truly wanted an open dialogue with the peoples of Central America, Henry Kissinger would not be named to head a fact-finding delegation. Progressive elements in Central America know Kissinger as the mastermind of the destabilization of the Allende government in Chile in 1973, and the architect of the destruction of Vietnam and Cambodia. Sending him to Central America is like sending Adolf Hitler to Israel.

During the aftermath of the CIA-directed mining of Nicaraguan harbors in the spring of 1984, the Reagan administration achieved what may be the ultimate arrogance. When Nicaragua took the U.S.A. to the World Court to protest the illegality of its actions to destabilize that country, the Reagan administration announced that it would not abide by World Court rulings pertaining to Central America for two years. The U.S.A. also contested the jurisdiction of the World Court to hear the case. In November the World Court ruled, 15–1, that it did have jurisdiction, and decided, 16–0, to hear the case, keeping in effect preliminary restraining orders issued in May 1984, that the U.S.A. must cease blocking or mining Nicaraguan ports, and refrain from jeopardizing Nicaraguan political independence by supporting military or paramilitary activities against the Sandinista government.

Moral authority is often a convenient cover for pursuing less than moral goals. For example, Kissinger adds a personal note at the end of the commission report, "that the United States extends military assistance to El Salvador *above all to serve vital American political and security interests*" (p. 130; italics added). Elsewhere the report makes clear that what is at stake in Central America is the need to assure the world that U.S. strategic (i.e., economic) interests will not be threatened anywhere:

> Beyond the issue of U.S. security interests in the Central American-Caribbean region, our credibility worldwide is engaged. The triumph of hostile forces . . . would be read as a sign of U.S. impotence [p. 93].

A second fundamental assumption of U.S. foreign policy is that *wherever change occurs without U.S. control, it is the work of communists who are tools of Moscow or Cuba.* The Council for Inter-American Security produced a paper on U.S. foreign policy commonly referred to as the Santa Fe Report. It illustrates the role ideology plays in determining foreign policy options:

> The young Caribbean republics situated in our strategic backyard face not only the natural growing pains of young nationhood, but the dedicated, irrepressible activity of a Soviet-backed Cuba to win ultimately total hegemony over this region. And this region . . . is the "soft underbelly of the United States." . . .
>
> Foreign policy is the instrument by which peoples seek to assure their survival in a hostile world. War, not peace, is the norm of international affairs. . . .
>
> Survival demands a new U.S. foreign policy. America must seize the initiative or perish. For World War III is almost over. The Soviet Union, operating under the cover of increasing nuclear superiority, is strangling the Western industrialized nations. . . .
>
> The Americas are under attack. Latin America, the traditional alliance partner of the United States, is being penetrated by Soviet power. The Caribbean rim and basin are spotted with Soviet surrogates and ringed with socialist states.[48]

Such ideological gibberish would be humorous if the consequences were not so deadly. Many U.S. politicians and citizens truly believe that the problem in Central America and elsewhere is communism—not hunger, not poverty, not death squads, not investments and aid that foster inequality, not landownership patterns, but communism. Other politicians have told me that they know that U.S. military policies in Central America and elsewhere cause hunger. However, as one member of Congress said to me: "Congress is imprisoned in the shadow of McCarthyism. To talk about hunger and U.S. military policy you must risk being called a communist. Not many of my colleagues are ready to do that."

Many sections of the report of the Kissinger Commission read like pages from a Fred Sherwood diary. It is as ideologically bound as the Santa Fe Report. The commission, which spent less than eight hours in Nicaragua, rarely refers to that country without such prejudicial terms as "Marxist-Leninist" or "totalitarian." Those who are fighting U.S.-supported governments in Central America the commission labels "totalitarian guerrillas." The term "Marxist-Leninist" appears ten times in the first five pages of the chapter on Central American security issues (pp. 84–88).

Carlos Andrés Perez, former president of Venezuela, in the fall of 1983 appealed to North Americans to change their paternalistic attitudes and policies vis-à-vis Central America:

> What North Americans don't understand is that in the long run we share a common fate—a past and a present that implicate North America in the skewed development and upheavals of the rest of the hemisphere. For decades, the United States baffled us with its unconditional support for Central American dictators—*so much so that many Latin Americans now suspect the word "democracy."* The dictators created exclusive societies based on systematic injustice—breeding grounds for explosive discontent. . . .
>
> Can't the United States see that conflict is inevitable in countries beseiged by poverty and political subjugation? . . .
>
> Our problems smolder, then burst into flame, but one thing remains constant: the unbearable paternalism of the United States and its apparent distrust of any Latin American with a sense of self-respect [italics added].[49]

The use and abuse of elections is one of the greatest tragedies of the long history of U.S. domination of Central America. Democratically elected governments deemed hostile to U.S. interests by elitist U.S. policy-makers have been ousted in Guatemala, Chile, and Jamaica by a combination of overt and covert means. In Guatemala and Chile the U.S. government was able to use and strengthen right-wing elements within the military to overthrow democratic systems and replace them with brutal military dictatorships.

One of the favorite U.S. criticisms of the Sandinistas is that they have a large army and a civilian militia. Few observers have noted that the Nicaraguan decision to maintain a strong military presence grew out of lessons learned from the U.S. use of the military in Guatemala and Chile to oust progressive governments. The Sandinistas concluded that there were two essential elements to keeping their revolution on course: (1) exercise power and pursue development in ways that involve the people and ensure its continued support, and (2) maintain a military presence as an integral part of the revolutionary process.

The U.S. use of the military to oust democratic leaders is only part of a tragic legacy. Equally alarming, the U.S. government has sponsored elections in Central America, not as a means by which a people can express democratic aspirations, but as a means to legitimize the militarization of the region. The military in both Honduras and El Salvador, the real power brokers in those countries, agreed to elections based on the assurance of increased military aid and with the understanding that their power would be enhanced as military hardware flowed into their countries after the elections. The militaries of Guatemala and Honduras should not be expected to reduce their power despite elections in both countries in late Fall, 1985. It is predictable, however, that the U.S. will seek to use these elections as a justification for greater economic and military aid.

Central American governments dominated by the military have used and abused elections for decades. The electoral techniques employed today are more subtle, as a result of U.S. involvement, but the results are largely the same. The policy of right-wing governments, including those of El Salvador and Guatemala, has been to systematically eliminate moderate professionals. Death squads, firmly rooted in the military, target doctors, teachers, religious and labor leaders, lawyers and centrist politicians for assassination. Progressive and radical leaders are also assassinated, and death squads use terror as a means of deterring popular participation in political action.

The elimination of the political center is part of a well-conceived strategy. Right-wing groups in and outside Central America believe that the U.S.A. will not tolerate another "leftist" victory. Hence they eliminate the center and force the U.S.A. to make a choice. The U.S. government can either accept more fundamental changes demanded by opposition groups, many of whom advocate changes consistent with the logic of the majorities, or it can stand by elements of the right. The U.S. government may wish to partially disengage itself from the treacherous right-wing death squads, which it has helped train, but it refuses to do so at the cost of fundamental democratization of societies that would elevate the poor to levels of decision-making. Therefore, the U.S.A. cooperates with elements of the right and rescues their image at election time, while labeling progressive individuals and groups "communists" and "subversives."

Allan Nairn, writing in the May 1984 edition of *The Progressive,* summarizes the U.S. role in the terror tactics that prevail in El Salvador:

> Early in the 1960s, during the Kennedy administration, agents of the U.S. government in El Salvador set up two official security organizations that killed thousands of peasants and suspected leftists over the next fifteen years. These organizations, guided by American operatives, developed into the paramilitary apparatus that came to be known as the Salvadoran death squads.
>
> Today, even as the Reagan administration publicly condemns the

death squads, the CIA—in violation of U.S. law—continues to provide training, support, and intelligence to security forces directly involved in death squad activity.

Interviews with dozens of current and former Salvadoran officers, civilians, and official American sources disclose a pattern of sustained U.S. participation in building and managing the Salvadoran security apparatus that relies on death squad assassinations as its principal means of enforcement. Evidence of U.S. involvement covers a broad spectrum of activity. [50]

The strategy of right-wing groups and governments to eliminate the political center appears to be working. The result of widespread terror and intimidation, economic inequality, and the assassination of political moderates is that the political center in many underdeveloped countries moves leftward. It is therefore unacceptable to the United States. The U.S. government, sometimes willingly, sometimes reluctantly, but always consistently, supports elements of the right wing. Ironically, by offering such support it continues to push the center leftward. The U.S. government opposes all those who will not allow it to manage change within their countries. They are, in the words of Carlos Andres Perez, persons with "a sense of self-respect" who want to determine their own destinies.

THE CHALLENGE OF THE MAJORITIES

Ideology is a formidable tool in the hands of U.S. policy-makers and a formidable obstacle to compassion. Ideological manipulation distorts the underlying causes of hunger and social turmoil. It separates us from our neighbors and robs U.S. citizens of the opportunity to learn from other peoples, other systems. Most important, ideological code words serve to cover up the fundamental frustration of many U.S. leaders: a loss of power to dictate events in other countries. Groups or governments which want to determine their own destinies are subject to a blitz of ideological code words. "Totalitarian," "Marxist-Leninist," "leftist," and "Cuban-backed" are terms used daily by the U.S. government and press in an ideological war to discredit those who want social change independent of U.S. manipulation. U.S. policy toward Nicaragua demonstrates how ideology can be used and abused in order to discredit the logic of the majorities.

I remember a meeting I had with Roger Gamble at the U.S. embassy in Nicaragua in June 1983. Mr. Gamble was second in command at the embassy. The U.S. press had documented CIA efforts to destabilize Nicaragua. CIA efforts were being complemented by a variety of economic pressures. The U.S. government transferred 90 percent of the Nicaraguan sugar quota to Honduras, instructed its representatives in multilateral lending institutions to oppose loans to Nicaragua, restricted food aid, and through a variety of military maneuvers pressed Nicaragua to divert resources from economic development to military preparation.

The question I put to Roger Gamble was simple: "Why? Why was the U.S.A. seeking to destabilize the Nicaraguan government?" His answer said more about why the U.S.A. should *not* destabilize Nicaragua than why it should. For example, he said, as had the U.S. ambassador, Anthony Quaintan, that the majority of Nicaraguans supported the Sandinistas and that in fair elections they would win. (This observation was confirmed in November 1984, when the Sandinistas received 63 percent of the vote in an election in which 75.5 percent of eligible voters voted.) He also said that the principal justification alleged for U.S. hostility toward Nicaragua was a red herring. "The amount of arms moving through Nicaragua to El Salvador," Gamble said, "is small. It shouldn't be an issue." (This point was later confirmed when David MacMichal, a CIA analyst in charge of gathering evidence on the alleged arms flow from Nicaragua to El Salvador, was not offered an extension of his contract after challenging Reagan administration distortions and fabrications on this issue.)[51]

When pressed, Roger Gamble finally admitted that the reason the Sandinista government had to be destroyed was because Nicaragua wanted to be free. "The problem with Nicaragua," Gamble said, "is that it doesn't understand geopolitics. The U.S. has always exerted a dominant influence over this area of the world and it always will. Nicaragua cannot ignore history." He then went on to draw this important analogy: "Just as Eastern Europe lives under the heavy thumb of the Soviet Union, so too Nicaragua has a big uncle looking over its shoulder. Nicaragua cannot ignore history."

The desire of the U.S. government to manage or dictate the affairs of other countries explains its hostility toward Nicaragua. The U.S. marines occupied Nicaragua from 1912 to 1925 and again from 1926 to 1933. A Nicaraguan peasant named Augusto César Sandino resisted the U.S. occupation. Sandino and his followers helped push the marines out in 1933 but not before the U.S.A. trained a powerful and repressive National Guard with Anastasio Somoza at its head. For nearly half a century the Somoza family dictatorship dominated Nicaragua with full support from the United States. The story of these years is one of terror, economic exploitation, and corruption.[52]

Franklin D. Roosevelt was once asked how the U.S.A. could support someone like Somoza. He said: "Somoza may be an s.o.b., but he's *our* s.o.b." The U.S. bought and militarily supported a faithful ally. Nicaragua rarely if ever voted against the U.S. in the United Nations, and it allowed the U.S.A. to use its land as a base from which to launch several paramilitary attacks against "unfriendly" governments in the region.

These stories say something about why the U.S. government sponsored the Somoza family dictatorship. There is another story that sheds light on the character of the dictators it supported. The Costa Rican government once showcased some its social accomplishments to the visiting Somoza. He visited health clinics, schools, and child nutrition centers. "We don't want this in Nicaragua," Somoza later told reporters, "We don't want people. We want oxen."

The vast majority of Nicaraguans throughout the years of the U.S.-backed Somoza dictatorship lived like oxen. They had little else but hope, a vision for the future. Edwin Castro, a Nicaraguan poet, captured this hope in a poem, "Tomorrow":

> The daughter of the worker,
> the daughter of the peasant, won't have to prostitute herself
> —bread and work will come from her honorable labor.
>
> No more tears in the homes of workers.
> You'll stroll happily over the laughter
> of paved roads, bridges, country lanes. . . .
>
> Tomorrow, my son, everything will be different;
> no whips, jails, bullets, rifles will repress ideas.
> You'll stroll through the streets of all the cities
> with the hands of your children in your hands—
> as I cannot do with you.
>
> Jail will not shut in your young years
> as it does mine;
> and you will not die in exile
> with your eyes trembling
> longing for the landscape of your homeland,
> like my father died.
> Tomorrow, my son, everything will be different.

Edwin Castro was murdered in 1960 in one of Somoza's jails. The signs of his vision are emerging for the first time in the new Nicaragua. I visited Nicaragua three times in 1982 and 1983. My wife and I moved there in 1984. It is a very poor country struggling to rebuild a society after years of exploitation under the U.S.-backed Somoza dictatorship. It is a country with many problems and yet it demonstrates in its infancy the possibilities of establishing the logic of the majorities as the foundation of economic planning and development. Unfortunately, it also illustrates how the forces of power, including that of the U.S.A., rise up in an effort to destroy the seeds of creative alternatives.

THE U.S.A. AND NICARAGUA

In Nicaragua the logic of the majorities, with its emphasis on the well-being of the poor, sufficiency, and equity, is deeply rooted in the Sandinista program.[53] This logic can easily be contrasted with the logic of capital identified with the U.S.-sponsored Somoza dictatorship. The economy under Somoza was characterized by Somoza's greed, co-option of other wealthy groups, corruption, concentration of wealth and power, brutal repression, and a classic agro-export system in which national foreign exchange earnings depended on a narrow range of agricultural exports. Somoza owned many of the largest businesses in Nicaragua, plus approximately 20 percent of the arable land. Inequalities were highly visible in both urban and rural areas. In the country-side between 60 and 70 percent of Nicaraguans were either landless or living on land too marginal to meet the needs of their families. *Campesinos* suffered from threefold repression: no land, no access to credit (only 16,000 of a possible 130,000 farm families received credit from Somoza-dominated banks for agriculture; the rest either received no credit or were subject to usury), and unfair prices. One measure of the tragic results of the U.S.-backed Somoza system was serious malnutrition. The U.S. Agency for International Development did a nutrition survey in 1976, which stated that "malnutrition is one of the most serious and widespread socio-economic problems in Nicaragua." It estimated that 56.6 percent of children under age 4 suffered from malnutrition.

The logic of capital had certainly taken its toll on the majority of the population. The Sandinistas inherited this legacy and other obstacles as well. The war had left fifty thousand Nicaraguans dead, Somoza had bombed numerous cities and factories, and much of the farmland had not been culti-vated during the fighting. Somoza left the country with a $1.6 billion debt (functionally the debt was much larger because little of the borrowed capital had gone into productive investment) and with approximately $3 million in the Central Bank (enough to pay government expenses for two days). The country also inherited the dependency of the agro-export economy, the structural inequality of the international economy, and the legacy of environmental abuse including contaminated lakes, deforestation (the virgin forests had been cut down by U.S. companies in the 1950s) and an agricultural system highly dependent on dangerous chemicals.

These initial obstacles were tempered somewhat by an international out-pouring of goodwill toward Nicaragua. In 1980 it received at least $700 million in reconstruction aid, including assistance from the United States. The Nicara-guans set out to organize their economic reconstruction based on the logic of the majorities, including a major effort to invest human and financial re-sources in the countryside where the majority of poor Nicaraguans live. The logic of the majorities is reflected in a number of programs and successes:

• The National Literacy Crusade launched in 1980 reduced illiteracy from approximately 50 to 12 percent. Nicaragua was unanimously chosen for first prize for its efforts by a panel of judges selected by UNESCO (the United Nations Educational, Scientific, and Cultural Organization).

• Nicaragua has achieved dramatic health improvements through various nationwide campaigns (disease immunizations) plus a major effort to expand free health services throughout the country. Polio has been eliminated, and malaria reduced by 75 percent. The infant mortality rate went down by a third after five years of revolution. Nicaragua has been singled out by the World Health Organization as a model country for primary health care.

• Nicaragua invested heavily in development of human capital through education. The number of schools doubled during the first five years of the revolution and the number of teachers from 12,500 to 41,500. In 1985 approximately 1.2 million Nicaraguans out of a total population of 3 million were attending school. This includes adults who are participating in programs to follow up on the literacy campaign.

• Improvements in housing have been achieved by government programs. Initially the government coupled free land titles with materials that were to be paid back over a 20-year period. Payments were to be determined by the income of each recipient. The U.S.-backed counterrevolutionary war has aggravated fiscal problems and seriously restricted resources so that these programs have been curtailed. However, land titles are still available and those who have this security are building and improving homes as they are able.

• A national distribution system ensures that all citizens receive basic items such as rice, beans, sugar, oil, and other commodities at government-regulated prices. This program is meant to provide a measure of food security to all Nicaraguans.

• These impressive efforts to improve literacy, education, health care, nutrition, and housing have been complemented by a land reform program. The program is pragmatic, consistent with the biblical logic of the majorities, and a significant factor in improving the lives of the rural population. By July 1985, approximately 70,000 land-poor families had received free title to nearly one-fourth of the arable land. *Campesinos* have received more than three million acres of land since 1979 and now own more than ten times the land held by *campesinos* at the time of Somoza. The land reform has also sought to reinforce the security of large, private holders who are committed to production. Both established producers and recent recipients of land have benefited from the Sandinista commitment to agriculture in keeping with the logic of the majorities. From 1978 through 1982 Nicaraguan capital investment in agriculture increased 309 percent. In Guatemala and Costa Rica, by way of contrast, investment in agriculture during the same period *declined* by 57 and 73 percent, respectively.

The accusation made by the Reagan administration, some rich Nicaraguans, and the Nicaraguan Catholic hierarchy against the Sandinista government is that it maintains a Marxist/Leninist, totalitarian state. It is certainly possible to find fault with the Sandinistas in terms of their original encounters with indigenous peoples, management of some aspects of the economy, and in other areas. However, ideologically-charged accusations of totalitarian Marxism-Leninism are absurd. More than 60 percent of the GNP is in private hands. Although Nicaraguan military aid comes primarily from the socialist bloc countries, it has set out to diversify its dependency in terms of economic relationships. During the time of Somoza nearly all Nicaraguan aid came from the U.S.A. and approximately 50 percent of Nicaraguan trade was with the United States. This economic dependency on the U.S.A. resulted in a high degree of political dependency and economic vulnerability.

The importance of diversifying its dependency by expanding and balancing its international economic relationships became starkly clear when President

Reagan imposed a trade blockade against Nicaragua in May 1985. From July 1979 through 1984 the largest aid givers to Nicaragua were Third World countries, followed by Western Europe and the socialist bloc. By the time of the U.S. trade blockade less than 17.5 percent of Nicaraguan commerce was with the U.S.A., 26 percent was with Western Europe, 20.5 percent with Latin America, 20 percent with socialist countries, 10 percent with Japan, and the remainder with a host of other countries.

The charge of totalitarian Marxism/Leninism fails to hold up in terms of internal dynamics as well. The Nicaraguan government has nationalized three important sectors, leaving the bulk of production in private hands. The nationalized sectors are natural resources (mining, forestry, and fishing), banking, and export/import trade. The control of banking and of the export/import trade is the most important in terms of government supervision of the economy. Control of banking allows the Nicaraguan government to direct credit to the poor majorities. For example, whereas only 16,000 farm families received bank credit for agriculture during the time of Somoza, more than 120,000 farm families receive credit today. Small farmers receive credit at lower interest rates than their larger, wealthier counterparts.

Control of the export/import trade gives the government access to dollars. The producers of basic export commodities—coffee, sugarcane, cotton— receive credit from the government but they must sell their products to the government. The government pays producers primarily in cordobas (the national currency of Nicaragua) and sells these commodities on the international market for dollars. Dollars that would otherwise be squandered by the rich for luxury consumption and trips to Miami are used instead to import medicines and materials needed for the economy, and to pay the interest on the national debt. The Nicaraguan government under the leadership of the Sandinistas is attempting to keep the majority of economic production in private hands, while exercising control of key economic sectors. This enables it to gradually reduce income differentials between the rich and the poor. The government is setting boundaries for an economy in which private producers become stewards of their own assets.

There are two things that infuriate the one-third to one-half of the large businesses in Nicaragua that are hostile to the revolutionary process. First, the rich are now largely part of the cordoba rather than the dollar economy. Their privileges as internationalists (producers and consumers in the global supermarket) are being eroded and they must become Nicaraguans. Secondly, in Nicaragua, unlike nearly every other country in the world, economic power does not automatically translate into political power. In Nicaragua many poor persons have significant political power. Many rich Nicaraguans are withholding economic investments even though they are able to make money in Nicaragua. They withhold investments in order to destabilize the Nicaraguan economy because they are buoyed by the commitment of the Reagan administration to overthrow the Nicaraguan government and thereby elevate Nicaraguan elites to their "rightful" place as political power brokers within the framework of a subservient relationship to the United States.

I suspect that a major reason for U.S. hostility toward Nicaragua is related to the Nicaraguan mixed economy and its diversified international relationships. The Nicaraguan economy is neither capitalist nor Marxist/Leninist, but a creative example of a mixed economy embodying socialist principles. U.S. military and economic policy toward Nicaragua seems determined to destroy the Nicaraguan experiment either by imposing a U.S. proxy government or by forcing Nicaragua to move closer to the Soviet bloc. Nicaragua will either fit U.S. categories or be the subject of unrelenting hostility.

Nicaragua is a threat because its independent existence fundamentally challenges the Monroe Doctrine and its premise that the U.S.A. has sovereignty over nations to the south. It is also a threat because this small country (approximately the size of Michigan) of 3 million persons is acting like a multinational company. Nicaraguan control of capital through nationalization of the banks, and control of markets through the nationalization of the export/import trade, is similar to the control exercised by multinationals. The difference, which is a profound one, is that the logic of capital applauds such control only when profits are distributed to private shareholders—often to the detriment of others. Nicaragua is acting like a multinational corporation, but using profits for its social programs based on the logic of the majorities. Therefore, from the perspective of the logic of capital, Nicaragua must be destroyed.

The next few years will be very difficult for Nicaragua. Its economy, like that of all its neighbors in Central America, is in shambles. Deteriorating terms of a trade, fiscal deficits, growing indebtedness, contra-inflicted war damage, diversion of resources from economic development to war preparation (military expenses equaled approximately 7 percent of the national budget in 1980, and more than 40 percent in 1985), a shortage of skilled managers, lagging private investment, and economic pressures from the U.S.A. (including a trade embargo) have started to erode some of the gains of the Nicaraguan revolution.

The U.S.-backed contra war targets health centers, schools, and farm cooperatives for destruction. Eighty percent of the basic foods of the country are produced in areas subject to contra activity. The three-year, 1982–84, period of strong U.S. support for the counterrevolutionary war caused an estimated $1 billion in economic losses for Nicaragua, including lost export revenues and damages to facilities and infrastructure. This was equivalent to between 70 and 80 percent of the value of export earnings over the same period. The war drains the emotions and the treasury of the country as it prepares to try to withstand the wrath of the giant to the north.

There are three predictable scenarios for the near future of Nicaragua:

• First, the U.S.A. will continue to expand the war of attrition. This will force Nicaragua to divert ever scarcer resources from social services and economic production to military use. The population will be mobilized for a survival economy (this in fact is already happening) and the hope will be to preserve the gains that have already been achieved rather than to expand them.

A survival economy will limit gains of the poor while further curtailing the privileges of the rich and middle classes. The Nicaraguan government is clear that from both a moral and biblical perspective, austerity should begin with the relatively well off, not with the poor. The Catholic hierarchy in Nicaragua disagrees and has become the voice of the upper classes. The sadistic goal of this war of attrition is to make the Nicaraguan people suffer so as to erode support from the Sandinista government.

• Or, secondly, the U.S.A. could launch a full-scale invasion of Nicaragua using U.S. and regional troops. If this happens, the leadership of the present Nicaraguan government will return to the mountains and a protracted guerrilla war will ensue. Hundreds of thousands of persons will die in a war that will likely become regional in scope.

• Or, thirdly, a regional peace treaty, such as that sought by the Contadora nations, could be signed and implemented. This would diffuse regional tensions and allow Nicaragua to return to the reconstruction of the country based on the logic of the majorities. The Nicaraguan economy would likely experience significant growth, coupled with a corresponding redistribution of wealth. It could also launch efforts to expand processing industries for commodities such as coffee and cotton and other basic industries, which would reduce dependency on the international economy. An authentic regional settlement involving the Central American countries and the sponsoring nations of Contadora could open up the possibility of regional economic integration along the lines of the United Nations plan subverted by the U.S.-backed Central American Common Market.

This third option is, sadly, the least likely, due to U.S. hostility. Nicaragua agreed to sign the Contadora agreement without revisions. This agreement would have resulted in the demilitarization of Central America by closing all foreign military bases and schools, ending international military maneuvers, removing all foreign military advisors, setting limits on the size of armies and the quality and quantity of arms, and would have ended support for insurgent groups in neighboring countries. The U.S. government refused to cooperate with this agreement and lobbied hard to get the Central American countries not to sign it, because its disarmament clauses would have reduced U.S. power in the region. In my view, the U.S. government is hostile to Contadora because it sets a dangerous precedent—Latin Americans solving their own problems—and thereby is a step toward the dismantling of the Monroe Doctrine.

The likelihood of a full-scale U.S. invasion should not be ruled out. However, the most likely scenario is that of an expanded war of attrition. The U.S.A. has the power to make life miserable for the Nicaraguan people, to aggravate internal pressures and tensions, and to discredit, at least in part, economic efforts based on the logic of the majorities. Malnutrition, shortages, and economic hardships are returning to Nicaragua. A Nicaraguan mother told a co-worker of mine as she breast-fed her child on a bus in northern Nicaragua, "I think your government enjoys playing with the stomachs of humanity."

The logic of the majorities is struggling to be born through a fledgling experiment in Nicaragua and through the hopes and aspirations of other courageous Central Americans. The questions put by Padre Pedro about who is for and who is opposed to this logic of the majorities should burn in the hearts of Christians in North America.

One of the tragic ironies of the Kissinger Commission report is its observation that "many Central Americans with whom we met emphasized the importance of bold initiatives to improve Central American living conditions." It then identified a list of "ambitious yet realistic objectives for the 1980s," which included the reduction of malnutrition, the elimination of illiteracy, universal access to primary health care and education, a significant reduction of infant mortality, and a significant improvement in housing (p. 68). These are precisely the goals and even successes of the Nicaraguan government that the U.S. government is trying to destroy! The lesson that U.S. citizens concerned about hunger and the logic of the majorities must learn is that Nicaragua has made significant progress in health, education, literacy, nutrition, and housing *only after overthrowing a U.S.-sponsored dictatorship and in the midst of continued economic and military harassment from the United States.* We must work to change U.S. policies designed to increase the suffering of the Nicaraguan people. We must also ensure that the U.S.A. does not distort history to the point that the logic of the majorities is discredited.

The peoples of Central America who are struggling against the weight of misguided U.S. policies are holy peoples. This is true not because they are perfect or sinless peoples—clearly they are not—but because their needless suffering raises a cry for repentance and compassion that offers them and their oppressors the possibility for healing, conversion, and redemption. The most obvious result of the failure to heed this cry is increased suffering for the peoples of Central America. Less obvious implications within the U.S.A. include continued erosion of democracy, greater internal repression, and a growing obsession with military power that threatens the destruction of the world as we know it.

It is beyond the scope of this book to explore all the dangers of U.S. foreign policy, but in the opinion of this author we are constructing a tragedy beyond our thinking because a small group of persons is allowed to define the "national interests of the United States," and to implement policies to defend them based in part on support derived through calculated lies and misinformation fed to the American public. Raymond Bonner in his book, *Weakness and Deceit*, has documented this problem in relation to the myths and reality undergirding U.S. policy in El Salvador.[54] The poor in Central America are suffering not only *from* the weight of U.S. arrogance and domination, they are also suffering *for* the liberation of the people and the nation responsible for their oppression. We shall either heed their call to repentance and compassion or we shall live with the historical consequences of our failure to do so.

Chapter 5

Disarming the Gods of Metal

The cry for compassionate action echoes from the voices of present and future generations of victims of the arms race. War preparation is the leading killer in our world today. Weapons do not have to be *used* to exact a deadly toll. The American Catholic bishops, in their pastoral letter on war and peace, *The Challenge of Peace,* have said that "the arms race is one of the greatest curses on the human race and the harm it inflicts upon the poor is more than can be endured" (p. 5).[55] If modern weapons of mass destruction *are used* they will likely cause catastrophic and irreversible ecological and genetic damage that will destroy life on earth (p. 32).

War preparations and the use of *conventional* weapons condemn millions of human beings to starvation, malnutrition, and economic injustice. Vital resources are squandered for military production and weapons are used in the service of unjust foreign policy goals that reinforce the skewed economies that cause hunger. *Nuclear* weapons supposedly guarantee security, but they threaten the destruction of present and future generations. The emotional and psychological effects of being nuclear hostages are devastating. Many young persons today are living without a sense of a future. A pastor told me about a discussion she had with the youth of her church. In response to a question about what they would be doing fifteen years from now, eighty percent of them said they would be dead. Other pastors have recounted similar experiences. The thought-provoking title of the Maryknoll film on the nuclear arms race, "Gods of Metal," captures the essence of the spiritual problem involved. Faith in nuclear weapons as the foundation of security undermines security that rests in faith in God. Nuclear bombs have become more than powerful weapons. They have become powerful idols that demand ultimate allegiance.

HOLY WARRIOR AND CRUCIFIED LORD

Those who look to the Bible for easy answers about how to compassionately respond to problems of violence, national security, and nuclear weapons are likely to be disappointed. The biblical teachings are conflictual. Quotations can be and often are used to justify almost any posture. God in the Old Testament is sometimes depicted as a holy warrior:

> God is often seen as the one who leads the Hebrews in battle, protects them from their enemies, makes them victorious over other armies. . . . This metaphor provided the people with a sense of security; they had a God who would protect them even in the face of overwhelming obstacles. It was also a call to faith and trust. . . . The warrior God was highly significant during long periods of Israel's understanding of its faith. But this image was not the only image, and it was gradually transformed, particularly after the experience of the exile, when God was no longer identified with military victory and might.[56]

The image of God as a holy warrior is totally absent from the New Testament. However, many Christians use it to justify a militaristic posture. Following a sermon I preached on peace during the Vietnam war, a man stormed up to me and said, "If you like peace then become a Quaker [we were both Lutheran]. I've read the Old Testament and God likes war."

Nonviolent resisters of evil can look to the cross of Christ and build a powerful case for the path they have chosen. The compassionate action of Gandhi, a non-Christian, and of Martin Luther King, Jr., were influenced by New Testament passages, for example,

> If your enemy is hungry, feed him; if he is thirsty, give him drink; for by so doing you will heap burning coals upon his head. Do not be overcome by evil, but overcome evil with good [Rom. 12:20–21].

James Douglass, through the examples of his life and writing, lends credibility to the nonviolent option. He writes in his compelling book, *The Nonviolent Cross*, that "revolution is not a question or a possibility" but "an obligation and a necessity." This is true because economic exploitation, hunger, and the threat of nuclear annihilation are intolerable for Christians. It is the *means* used by revolutionaries, not the necessity of revolution, that concerns Douglass:

> But given its inspiration in a cry of the living for the life they were created for, revolution cannot then bridge the living and the life they seek by a sword. It cannot fulfill life through death. It cannot create a new order of justice by murdering all those who supported injustice, for injustice will have merely changed hands.[57]

It is difficult to reconcile the cross with violence. However, Christians have done so for centuries. "The Christians say they love Christ," says Ernie Levy, a character in André Schwarz-Bart's novel *The Last of the Just*, "but I think they hate him without knowing it. So they take the cross by the other end and make a sword out of it and strike us with it."

There can be little doubt that based on New Testament teaching the preferred option for confronting evil is nonviolent resistance. Many thoughtful Christians refuse to justify militaristic policies on the basis of the Old Testament image of God as a holy warrior. However, they also reject the nonviolent cross as normative for Christian behavior, because it seems an inadequate response to the depth of evil that must be confronted in situations such as Nazi Germany, Soviet intervention in Afghanistan, or U.S.-sponsored repression in Latin America. The Catholic bishops in their pastoral letter on war and peace state the dilemma between Christian teaching on nonviolence and the reality of evil:

> We believe work to develop nonviolent means of fending off aggression and resolving conflict best reflects the call of Jesus both to love and to justice. . . . But, on the other hand, the fact of aggression, oppression, and injustice in our world also serves to legitimate the resort to weapons and armed force in defense of justice. We must recognize the reality of the paradox we face as Christians living in the context of the world as it presently exists; we must continue to articulate our belief that love is possible and the only real hope for all human relations, and yet accept that force, even deadly force, is sometimes justified [p. 25].

Christians living in Central America have reluctantly taken up arms against U.S.-backed dictatorships. I have had numerous conversations with Christians in Nicaragua who described life under Somoza and their decision to participate in military action. Land in Nicaragua was controlled by an elite, infant mortality was high, malnutrition was widespread, and there was no medical care available for the vast majority of the population. Women, children, husbands, and wives were taken from their homes and tortured or killed without provocation by members of Somoza's national guard. Nonviolent means of protest such as petitions to government leaders, demonstrations, and other public protests were brutally repressed. The decision of many Christians to couple violent means with other forms of protest was painful yet seemingly inevitable. The same is true today. Although it is possible that efforts such as that of the Contadora nations could reduce regional tensions and thereby lessen the need for military defense, it would be virtually impossible, within the framework of U.S. hostility, for the Sandinistas to survive more than a few days or months without military preparedness. Military preparedness is no guarantee that the Sandinistas will stay in power. But without military preparation they would have been ousted immediately, along with their economic example based on the logic of the majorities.

Phillip Berryman in his excellent book on Christians in Central American revolutions concludes that nonviolent options are insufficient to bring about fundamental social changes:

> In Central America [in contrast to the American civil rights movement]. . . the demands of the poor are not absorbable—at this point they demand a restructuring of the economy, which at the very least will end the existence of a true oligarchy and severely curtail the style of

life of the privileged, as well as including a new political order, starting with the dismantling (or thorough restructuring) of present armies, police, and paramilitary groups. It should come as no surprise, then, that existing power structures are willing to go to such lengths (massive killing tending toward genocide) to defend their privileges and status. From their viewpoint, the reaction is appropriate.

There would seem to be no historical precedent for true revolutions achieved through nonviolence. . . . For my part, then, I doubt that in the present circumstances nonviolent means would be sufficient for bringing about the kind of revolution needed in Central America.[58]

It is also not true that use of military force to overcome oppression automatically results in the murder of all who supported past injustices or that injustice will merely change hands, as James Douglass fears. For example, the Sandinistas, many of whom are Christian, took up arms against the Somoza dictatorship. Upon taking power, they immediately abolished the death penalty. They also released thousands of ex-Somoza national guardsmen from prison as part of a Christmas amnesty in 1980. Many of those released responded to this compassionate gesture by going to Honduras where they formed a counter-revolutionary group with assistance from the United States. Tomás Borge, the only surviving founder of the Sandinista front, was brutally tortured in Somoza's jails. His wife, too, was tortured, and died as a result of it. Borge became the Nicaraguan minister of the interior following the defeat of Somoza. He became a leader in the development of alternative, open prisons in Nicaragua. Many observers trace the absence of torture among prisoners in Nicaragua to the experiences of Sandinista leaders who were themselves tortured and thus recognize the importance of humane treatment.

The use of military force does not eliminate the need or possibility for nonviolent means of resistance. Hundreds of thousands of Nicaraguans who did not fight with guns provided food, shelter, and logistical support for those who did. Others participated in strikes and demonstrations. It was a combination of violent and nonviolent means of resistance that toppled Somoza. Nicaragua since 1979 has had to defend itself militarily. At the same time, thousands of persons from the U.S.A. and other countries have come to Nicaragua to participate in programs such as Witness for Peace and to work with coffee and cotton brigades. Through these programs international volunteers go to areas of conflict such as the border with Honduras and key agricultural areas subject to contra intervention. Their presence has greatly reduced the terrorism of the contras. Witness for Peace is a powerful form of nonviolent resistance to U.S.-sponsored aggression against Nicaragua.

There are two insights that can help keep this discussion in perspective. First, *questions about violence and nonviolence are important but they are not the only important questions for Christians.* The bottom line is that we must resist injustice and build peace. The means by which we resist injustice and build peace raise important moral and ethical issues. However, our call to be peacemakers is certain. Compassionate actions on behalf of peace and justice are often costly. They should be subject to intense criticism and reflection. Both violent and nonviolent means of protest should be offered up to God in a spirit of humility, acknowledging the fallibility of our discernment and our need for forgiveness.

Secondly, *Christians in the U.S.A. desperately need to expand their understanding of violence.* Amos condemns the wealthy in Israel who "store up violence and robbery in their strongholds" (Amos 3:10). Jeremiah confronts a king with the charge that the poor are denied justice while he practices "oppression and violence" (Jer. 22:17). Killing someone with a weapon is not the only form of violence. The violence condemned by the prophets permeated society. Hunger, poverty, inequality, repression, torture, and economic exploitation are forms of violence that block compassion and murder both bodies and spirits.

Sin expressed as violence against the poor becomes embodied in social structures. Violence is institutionalized by systems that concentrate landholdings, wealth, and power. In this regard, a pure nonviolent option is impossible. All of us who participate in systems that oppress the poor are stained with the blood of violence. Is there a meaningful moral distinction between shooting someone and tolerating the massive exportation of weapons to repressive governments? Is it better to promote economic policies that cause children to starve than to resist such policies by violent means? I think not.

Christians living in the U.S.A. must overcome the affliction of tolerating violence in service to U.S. corporate interests while condemning the violence of those who resist such oppression. "I would assert that people who have not actively opposed the violence of the powerful against the poor, at some cost to themselves," writes Berryman, "have no moral authority to question the violence used by the poor." It is the "spiral of violence," a term coined by Brazilian archbishop, Dom Helder Câmara, that must be broken. The first violence is the suffering of the poor caused by malnutrition, poverty, and the systems that perpetuate these injustices. The second violence is when the poor and others use force to resist and confront the individuals and systems that lock them into poverty and exploitation. The third violence is the military response from the rich and powerful who resort to repression in order to maintain systems of injustice. This completes the cycle and insures its continuation.

Our response to the nuclear threat, to problems of personal, national, and military security, and to questions about resistance, will be better informed if we affirm the pursuit of justice and peace as essential components of Christian compassion. Peace and justice depend on our commitment to uproot the structures of violence that permeate our lives and the world economy.

FIVE BIBLICAL INSIGHTS

The biblical message *is* both conflictual *and relevant* for Christians who struggle to respond compassionately to issues of war and peace. There are five biblical insights that can shape our understanding and action.

First, *the early church boldly affirmed that Christ is Lord.* Our ultimate allegiance is to Christ, not to the nation-state. The fundamental confusion within most churches in the U.S.A. is between patriotism and faith. Love of God and country are often equated. The U.S.A. is seen as a beacon of light resisting the evils of atheistic communism. These images are part of our history and our daily vocabulary. They are captured in the following quote from a U.S. senator near the turn of the century:

> God has . . . made us *the master organizers of the world* to establish system where chaos reigns. He has given us *the spirit of progress* to overwhelm the forces of reaction throughout the earth. He has made us adept in government that we may administer government among savage and senile peoples. Were it not for such a force as this, the world would relapse into barbarism and night. And of all our race He has marked the American people as *His chosen nation* to finally lead in the regeneration of the world. This is *the divine mission of America*, and it holds for us all the profit, all the glory, all the happiness possible to man. . . . What shall history say of us? Shall it say that we renounced that holy trust, left the savage to his base condition, the wilderness to the reign of waste, deserted duty, abandoned glory? No! They founded no paralytic government, . . . they unfurled no retreating flag. That flag has never paused in its onward march. Who dares halt it now—now, when history's largest events are carrying it forward? [italics added].[59]

There is a growing debate in the United States about restoring prayer in public schools as a means of promoting Christian values within the nation. I would argue that a much more significant step toward resurrecting Christian values would be the removal of U.S. flags, and the uncritical allegiance they symbolize, from our churches. *We are not American Christians.* We are Christians who find ourselves by accident of birth of circumstance to be living within the United States of America. When our commitment to Christ, including our work for the liberation of the poor, conflicts with the values, goals, economic priorities, or military policies of the nation, then resistance to the state is an obligation.

I have spoken to many "American Christians" about Central America. They refuse to explore charges of U.S. support for repression and underdevelopment in the region. They associate criticism of the nation with criticism of God! This uncritical patriotism blocks compassion, spiritual wholeness, and economic justice. It is a sign of idolatry. Criticism of the country is a criticism of their god, the nation-state.

The fact that we are Christians living in the U.S.A. does not mean that all forms of nationalism or patriotism are demonic or that Christians have no responsibilities to the nation. There are many things to appreciate about this country and part of Christian stewardship is to bring kingdom values to bear on national priorities through our involvement as citizens. However, our ultimate allegiance to God must be clear. The uncritical support that many

Christians lend to U.S. economic and military policies distorts compassion. Our support for policies that crush priorities based on the logic of the majorities indicates that we have failed in word and deed to affirm that Christ is Lord.

When Jesus was brought before Pilate his accusers said, "We found this man perverting our nation, and forbidding us to give tribute to Caesar" (Luke 23:2). When Pilate asks the chief priests whether he should crucify Jesus, the king of the Jews, they respond: "We have no king but Caesar" (John 19:15). Jesus is crucified by those whose faith is undermined by their refusal to confront Caesar. The god of nationalism continues to uproot compassion and to exact a deadly toll. Millions of persons suffer hunger and poverty caused or aggravated by the corporate and military practices of the United States. Our faith tells us that Jesus suffers with them. Jesus' call to compassionate action requires us to choose between repentance and uncritical allegiance to Caesar.

A second biblical insight is that *Christians should be committed to the well-being of the family of God, not only or principally to the nuclear family.* Jesus broadens the traditional notion of family:

> Then his mother and his brothers came to him, but they could not reach him for the crowd. And he was told, "Your mother and your brothers are standing outside, desiring to see you." But he said to them, "My mother and my brothers are those who hear the word of God and do it" [Luke 8:19–21].

Doing the word of God means embracing a broader family of believers. It also means reaching out with compassion and love to an ever widening circle of persons: Jews and gentiles, women and men, rich and poor, and all those in need of healing and transformation. This mission to and with the family of God is conflictual. Jesus expects it to divide nuclear families:

> Do not think that I have come to bring peace on earth; I have not come to bring peace, but a sword. For I have come to send a man against his father, and a daughter against her mother, and a daughter-in-law against her mother-in-law; and a person's foes will be those of their own household. He who loves father or mother more than me is not worthy of me; and he who loves son or daughter more than me is not worthy of me; and he who does not take up his cross and follow me is not worthy of me [Matt. 10:34–38].

Our narrow understanding of family stifles compassion. It is not that we should ignore the needs of our immediate family but that we need to see their needs in relation to the broader needs of the human family. "It is right and proper that we should have a particular love of our 'immediate family,'" writes Dom Helder Câmara, "the human group which gave us life."[60] Whatever conditions you live in, he urges us, care for you and yours but refuse to be locked within the narrow circle of your immediate family: decide to take on the whole family of humankind. Kathleen and James McGinnis in their wonderful book *Parenting for Peace and Justice* describe how family ministry can be linked to social ministry. The nuclear family is perhaps the most important place for value formation where creative links between justice in the family and global justice can be forged.[61]

The Bible suggests that we are all members of one family united by God's love. We often restrict family to blood ties. The tragedy of doing so is evident in a typical Christmas in the United States. We shower gifts on brothers and sisters, sons or daughters, moms and dads, grandchildren and grandparents, who often already have more things than they need. The meaning of Christmas, including the significance of the birth of Jesus and our commitment to the family of God, gets lost in the shuffle of gifts between family members. Our family spending spree is accompanied by indifference to the millions of human beings within the broader family of God who have little or nothing. The birth of Jesus is heralded as a saving event—for U.S. business. Our collective Christmas bill for 1983 was $125 billion.[62] *This is nearly twice the combined GNP of the thirty-one poorest countries ($63 billion) with a total population of 287 million.*[63]

There is no doubt that love is legitimately expressed through gift-giving. However, gift-giving often substitutes for genuine expressions of human love and caring. One danger of an overtly materialistic culture is that emotions and feelings are sidestepped through the giving and consumption of goods. The result is a double tragedy. Preoccupation with materialistic things stifles authentic love, communication, and caring. It ignores at the same time the needs of the broader family of God, including millions of persons who lack the bare necessities of life. On our way to buy a color television or video game, few of us would walk past a family member who is starving. However, we routinely do so when it comes to the broader family of God, which is our true family. It is revealing that groups like the Moral Majority focus so much attention on the nuclear family while ignoring Christian responsibility to the broader family of God.

Our views on security and war preparation are often influenced by whether our primary commitment is to the family of God or to the nuclear family. I know many parents who are concerned about U.S. policy in Central America because they have seen and felt the needless hunger and malnutrition of children throughout the region. They channel their feelings through the bonds they share with their own children. This often leads to outrage, commitment, and compassionate action.

I know other parents, particularly mothers, who became involved in antinuclear organizing because they want their children and other children to live with a sense of a future. A suburban housewife told me the story of how she became involved in peacemaking and how her motives for involvement expanded over time. Her 7-year-old son returned from school frightened on several successive days. "Mommy," he asked, "are we going to have a nuclear war?" Each day she responded, "No, we're not going to have a nuclear war. It's nothing for you to worry about." Later in the week her 5-year-old daughter woke up screaming in the middle of the night. She had dreamt that her mother and father were killed in a great war. "Mommy," she pleaded, "are we going to have a nuclear war?" "No," her mother said, "we're . . . ," and then she stopped. She could not finish the sentence. "I realized," she told me later, "that while my children should not have to worry about nuclear war, I did. If I told them not to worry about nuclear war, then I had to start working to prevent one."

This suburban housewife got involved because she was concerned about the fears and future of *her* children. However, she soon realized that nuclear war threatened *all* children. She also came to see that preparation for nuclear war was already killing millions of children by squandering precious resources. Her understanding about how her family fitted in with the broader family of God deepened both her faith and her commitment as a peacemaker.

A narrow commitment to the nuclear family can result in a selfish and uncritical acceptance of weapons production as the means to security. I know many families who support an escalating U.S. weapons budget because they see it as the way to protect their privileged lifestyles and way of life. "My family is comfortable and we've worked hard for what we have. Nobody is going to take it away from us." This common attitude reflects a narrow commitment to the nuclear family—a commitment linked to the threat of nuclear war. The nuclear umbrella promises to protect a way of life. The nuclear family becomes a family committed to a nuclear balance of terror.

A third insight is that *within the Bible there is an emerging understanding that the kingdom of God is distinct from any nation-state.* The period of Israelite history that included the exodus from Egypt and the journeys in the wilderness clearly associated the kingdom of God with God and the people of God. The Israelites were travelers and sojourners with God. This nomadic people entered the promised land and soon the kingdom of God was identified with the state of Israel. This notion of the kingdom as linked to a specific place was shattered by the experience of the exile. Israel lost its national identity as it left the promised land and was scattered throughout many nations. There were expectations throughout New Testament times that a Messiah would come and reestablish the nation of Israel as God's kingdom. The Zealots looked for such a Messiah even as they engaged in armed rebellion against the Roman empire. However, Jesus and the early church reinforced the understanding that the kingdom of God is distinct from any nation-state. The inbreaking of the kingdom had historical consequences, but it was associated with God and the people of God who work to embody kingdom values of justice, compassion, peace, and hope in all areas of life, cutting across barriers of race, sex, and nationality.

This distinction between God's kingdom and a given nation-state is a further reminder to Christians living in the U.S.A. of the importance of affirming the lordship of Christ. The U.S.A. is as far away from the kingdom as other countries. It desperately needs to be confronted and challenged by Christians who seek to be a leaven of compassion and justice in order to foster personal, national, and global priorities. It may be that we have special responsibilities as in the midst of a world power. Our faith journey must be ɔntext of the imperial ambitions and economic empire of the

ɔrs are rarely kind to empires. Egypt, Assyria, Babylon, and ɔɔcive harsh words. These empires often treated peoples of faith ɪiarshly. The Israelites were enslaved and oppressed by the Egyptians. Christians who refused military service and emperor worship were routinely fed to the lions by the Roman empire. The common biblical view of empires is likely to make the blood of "American Christians" boil when applied to our situation. The U.S.A. is not God's chosen nation any more than is the Soviet Union. In fact, as empires both countries pose enormous obstacles to kingdom values.

Christians in the U.S.A. need to perceive the nation in dramatically different ways. The need to do so can be illustrated with a simple example. The exodus drama is a favorite among oppressed and landless peoples in Central America. Moses, prodded by God, confronts the pharaoh. "Let my people go" becomes a rallying cry heard throughout many generations. The story of God's liberating activity in behalf of an oppressed people and the defeat of a powerful empire fills the poor with hope and courage. The rub for Christians living in the U.S.A. is that we often read the story and associate the U.S.A. with Moses. The poor of Central America read the story and associate the U.S.A. with the pharaoh!

A fourth biblical insight is that, although the institution of government is seen as a gift from God, *not all governments or governmental policies deserve allegiance or support from Christians.* The Israelites functioned without formal government when they were a nomadic people. They rejected human government as an affront to the sovereignty of God. For example, during the period of the judges the people of Israel tried to make Gideon their ruler:

> Then the Men of Israel said to Gideon, "rule over us, you and your son and your grandson also; for you have delivered us out of the hand of Midian." Gideon said to them, "I will not rule over you, and my son will not rule over you; the Lord will rule over you" [Judg. 8:22–23].

The Israelites eventually came to have their own government, usually in the form of a king, after they settled into the land and among the nations. However, kings were obliged to serve as instruments of God's justice. If they oppressed the poor, then they were harshly judged and they lost claim to any legitimate authority:

> Woe [death] to him who builds his house by unrighteousness, and his upper rooms by injustice; who makes his neighbor serve him for nothing, and does not give him his wages; who says, "I will build myself a great house with spacious upper rooms," and cuts out windows for it, paneling it with cedar, and painting it with vermilion. Do you think you are a king because you compete in cedar? Did not your father eat and drink and do justice and righteousness? Then it was well with him. He judged the cause

of the poor and needy; then it was well. Is not this to know me? says the Lord. But you have eyes and heart only for your dishonest gain, for shedding innocent blood, and for practicing oppression and violence [Jer. 23:13–17].

O my people, your leaders mislead you, and confuse the course of your paths. . . . The Lord enters into judgment with the elders and princes. . . . "It is you who have devoured the vineyard, the spoil of the poor is in your houses. What do you mean by crushing my people, by grinding the face of the poor?" says the Lord God of hosts [Isa. 3:12, 14–15].

The acceptance of government as superior to anarchy continues throughout both the exile and New Testament times. The legitimacy of government is not questioned but specific governments and governmental actions are resisted. Romans 13, which encourages Christians to "be subject to the governing authorities" and "also pay taxes," is often used as a blanket mandate for Christians to obey and finance all governmental authority. This view elevates the authority of government to that of God and must be rejected as idolatrous. The proclamation that Christ is Lord means that all allegiance given to the state or to other authorities is given provisionally, always subject to the condition that such allegiances do not contradict the lordship of Christ. Christians who eagerly cite Romans 13 should be required to read Revelation 13, which, although written in code, is a clear appeal for Christian resistance to the Roman empire.

The Christian perspective on the role of government can be clarified by a simple analogy. Imagine that there is a single well that provides water for the needs of fifty families. The well can be used only by one family at a time. The existence of anarchy insures that there is no coordination of who uses the well, when, or for what purpose. The potential benefits from the well are wasted as numerous conflicts arise. These problems encourage representatives from each of the fifty families to elect a council of ten to draw up regulations for determining use of the well. These regulations are adopted by the group. The council of ten, with the consent of the others, is given power to enforce regulations, monitor use, and collect taxes to finance the work of the council and to pay maintenance costs. The system works smoothly until council members decide to use the well to drown all children with dimples. Christians and others with human decency at this point refuse to accept the authority of the council. They must do all they can to prevent the atrocities and to change the members and policies of the council. Christians would have an obligation to resist the authority of the council even if a majority of the families agreed to expand the power of the council to include using the well to drown children with dimples.

The biblical perspective is that it is better to manage or govern the use of the well than it is to let anarchy prevail. A governing council or some similar authority is harmonious with God's intentions. However, *this* council must be resisted. Christians have no option but to resist the authority of the council, including withholding financial support, because killing children with dimples is an affront to Christian faith. Paul is correct when he says that Christians should pay taxes to legitimate governing authorities. However, Jesus says that we are to "render to Caesar the things that are Caesar's and to God the things that are God's" (Luke 20:25). Paying taxes is legitimate only so long as it does not violate the lordship of Christ. I affirm as a Christian and as a citizen of the U.S.A. that government is superior to anarchy. However, it is an obligation for me to resist the authority of the U.S. government when it conflicts with Christian faith and the lordship of Christ.

A fifth biblical insight is that *security is more than military power, and an overreliance upon military power can undermine security.* The biblical writers nearly always associate security with faithfulness to God and with justice to the poor. There is not true security apart from shalom, which means "peace" but has deeper meaning. Peace is sometimes thought of as the absence of war. It is conceivable within this framework to have peace while millions of persons starve to death. The essence of shalom is a peace that grows out of the economic and spiritual health of individuals and communities and their harmonious relationship within the whole of creation. Authentic peace and security depend on shalom.

Military power is often used to block compassion and reinforce the absence of shalom. The use of weapons to protect unjust privileges or power relationships that victimize the poor is condemned by Amos and Hosea. The rich are economically and militarily secure during the time of Amos. They build two-story, protective mansions as part of the defense system of the city. These strongholds protect their unjust wealth earned by exploiting the poor:

> "They do not know how to do
> right," says the Lord,
> "those who store up violence and
> robbery in their strongholds."
> Therefore thus says the Lord God:
> "An adversary shall surround the land,
> and bring down your defenses from you,
> and your strongholds shall be plundered"
> [Amos 3:10–11].

I discussed earlier how nationalism and patriotism can be idols that block compassion and violate the lordship of Christ. The wealthy of Israel think of themselves as "the notable people of the first of the nations" (Amos 6:1). They take great pleasure as Amos attacks the injustice of neighboring countries (Amos 1–2). However, their pleasure turns to anger as Amos continues his attack against their country. Amos condemns the use of military power to defend unjust privileges and idolatrous nationalism. Military power, itself an idol, is used to defend other idols.

The prophet Hosea, who followed Amos, clearly states how overreliance

upon military power and the use of military power to defend injustice undermine security that depends on justice and obedience to God:

> Sow for yourselves righteousness,
>> reap the fruit of steadfast love,
>> break up your fallow ground,
>> for it is time to seek the Lord,
>> that He may come and rain salvation on you.
> You have plowed iniquity,
>> you have reaped injustice,
>> you have eaten the fruit of lies.
> *Because you have trusted in your chariots*
> *and in the multitude of your warriors,*
> *therefore the tumult of war shall arise among your people,*
> *and all your fortresses shall be destroyed*
>> [Hos. 10:12–14; italics added].

Our call to be peacemakers is clear. It is indefensible from the perspective of
the Bible to participate in military systems that victimize the poor and feed
nationalistic idols. Micah envisions a time of shalom in which swords will be
beaten into plowshares and persons will be economically secure, unafraid
beneath their vines and fig trees (Micah 6:1–4). This vision and hope for the
future is contradicted by the absence of shalom so obvious in our world of
hunger, poverty, and the threat of nuclear holocaust.

THE MAGNITUDE, CAUSES, AND CONSEQUENCES
OF THE ARMS RACE

All the world would be well fed if missiles were edible. There are more
pounds of explosive power than pounds of food available today. Military
expenditures are high and increasing rapidly. The U.S. Arms Control and
Disarmament Agency estimates that world military spending increased from
less than $300 billion in 1972 to $820 billion in 1982. In 1985 spending for
weapons and other military purposes was expected to reach $1 trillion.[64] The
Worldwatch Institute reports that the value of weapons imports by underdeveloped countries now exceeds that of grain imports: "Developing countries
imported armaments in 1980, worth some $19.5 billion, and wheat and coarse
grains valued at $19.45 billion." The Religious News Service reported in early
1984:

> During the years following 1979, a period distinguished by lack of
> economic progress, the militarization of the world economy has accelera-
> ted, almost as though mounting economic stresses were causing political
> leaders to try to offset these insecurities by spending more on weapons.[65]

The U.S.A. and the Soviet Union are the engines of the global arms race.
Their fascination with military power hurts their own citizens even as it

victimizes the poor of other countries. The Soviet Union, which spent $1.3 trillion between 1960 and 1981 for military purposes, now ranks 25th among 142 countries in economic and social performance.[66] U.S. military spending totaled approximately $2 trillion over the 35-year period from 1945 to 1980. The U.S.A. will nearly match that amount in just *five* years, 1985 to 1989. This $2 trillion expenditure will cost the average taxpayer nearly $20,000 in taxes.[67]

It is almost impossible to comprehend the significance of spending $2 trillion. I made the following calculation and comparison to see how much money it really is. The U.S. national debt in the spring of 1984 was approximately $1.5 trillion. The debt is the result of government spending, largely for military purposes, that exceeded tax revenues. *If the U.S.A. were to balance the budget* (equalize government spending and taxes) *and pay off $1.5 trillion at the rate of $1 million a day, the debt would be paid in the year 6093, a period of 4,110 years* (assuming no interest payments). By way of comparison, *if U.S. military expenditures were reduced by 50 percent, we could pay off the entire national debt by 1992.*

The arms race is fed by a combination of fear, contorted economics, and illusion. The Soviet Union had more than 20 million citizens killed during World War II. This memory of death and destruction is clearly etched into the Soviet psyche and is reflected in the commitment to maintain a buffer of "friendly" nations (Eastern Europe) between itself and the West and to match U.S. military expenditures. The foreign policies of both countries, including Soviet intervention in Afghanistan and U.S. support for dictatorships in Central America, South Korea, and the Philippines, feed mutual suspicions and fears. Each new weapons system produced by either country is matched by the other in a seemingly endless spiral that increases tensions and the likelihood of nuclear war.

The Pentagon and weapons producers in the U.S.A. manipulate fear in order to serve their interests. We are generally not fearful enough around budget appropriations time and so with great fanfare they announce the discovery of a bomber gap, missile gap, megatonnage gap, or window of vulnerability. They are either lying to us and the threat is not nearly as imminent as they suggest (I suspect this is true) or they refuse to acknowledge the absurdity of repeating an approach that fails year after year (I suspect this is also true). They use fear in either case to convince us that the best way to put out the fire of the arms race is to continue pouring gasoline on it.

This charade would be comical if it were not so deadly. The government line takes a different twist if we become too fearful and take our protests to the streets. We are then subjected to the Pentagon balancing act of imminent threat and easy recovery. If we do not sell our souls and produce more destabilizing weapons, we are doomed. However, if there is a nuclear war, we should not worry too much because surviving a nuclear war is as simple as having a shovel. "Everybody's going to make it if there are enough shovels to go around," writes T. K. Jones, deputy under secretary for strategic and theater nuclear forces. "Dig a hole, cover it with a couple of doors and then throw three feet of dirt on top. It's the dirt that does it."[68]

The Pentagon and individual branches of the military do more than carry out public relations to manage fear. They lobby hard for increased military spending. Each new weapons system expands their power and influence. *The U.S. navy budget is larger than the combined governmental budgets of all twelve South American nations. The U.S. air force budget exceeds that of all forty-six African governments combined.*[69]

The lobbying efforts of corporations with military contracts complement those of the Pentagon. I suggested in chapter 3 that dollars and cents often muddle common sense and block compassion. Hunger is a significant problem because it is profitable. The same is true with the arms race. Economic considerations fuel the arms race in three ways. First, many workers depend on jobs in the military sector to provide income for their families. They often become uncritical lobbyists for large military expenditures. Secondly, the worldwide defense of unjust economic relationships depends on an aggressive foreign policy that includes assistance, arms sales, and military intervention. Finally, and most important, the arms race is fueled by the enormous profits that are made by military contractors.

Some of the largest corporations in the U.S.A. benefit most from large military expenditures. They receive on average, according to a U.S. government report, twice the profits of civilian industries.[70] The excessive profits built into military contracts constitute the largest welfare program in human history. Recipients are not the poor or the destitute but the rich and the powerful. Senator William Roth (R-Delaware), among others, has provided a number of examples of Pentagon generosity and corporate profiteering. A nut used in the F-18 jet has a market value of 13¢; the Pentagon price, $ 2,228. An antenna motor pin used in the F-16 has a market value of 2.4¢; the Pentagon price, $7,417.[71] These examples of profiteering can be extended to entire weapons systems. Many weapons systems are produced because they are profitable, not because they enhance security or lessen the likelihood of conventional or nuclear war.

Military contractors often claim to be carrying out rather than influencing government policies related to war production. However, their lobbying efforts belie their claims. Honeywell, for example, has been the target of significant public protest, including civil disobedience. It defended its war contracts with a full-page advertisement in the *Minneapolis Tribune*. The advertisement said in part:

> Honeywell does not take a political position on the level of the defense budget or on any specific defense programs. We do not think any corporation should be asked to, in effect, determine the country's defense policies.[72]

Honeywell, like many other war contractors, is not nearly as neutral as it pretends. It influences governmental and military policies through political action committees, a full-time registered lobbyist in Washington, D.C., membership in numerous trade associations that represent military contractors, and participation in federal advisory committees that provide input to the defense department. A survey by *Armed Forces Journal International* in 1980 indicated that the Honeywell Washington, D.C., office employs more than a thousand persons, eight hundred of them in defense-related areas.[73]

The chilling new dimensions of the nuclear arms race are the development of first-strike weapons and the illusion that nuclear war is not only survivable but winnable. Secretary of Defense Weinberger stated in a report detailing a 5-year defense plan that U.S. forces must be capable of "controlled nuclear counter-attacks over a protracted period" in order to "prevail and be able to force the Soviet Union to seek earliest termination of hostilities on terms favorable to the United States."[74] The Federal Emergency Management Agency reported in 1981 that "a close look at the facts shows with fair certainty that with reasonable protective measures, the United States could survive nuclear attack and go on to recovery within a relatively few years."[75]

The deterrent against nuclear war was until recently the acceptance of mutual assured destruction (MAD). Neither superpower would risk a nuclear attack that would prompt a devastating retaliatory response. The goal of deterrence was simply to have sufficient capability to absorb a nuclear attack and retaliate. First-strike weapons are entirely different. They are not designed to deter the use of nuclear weapons. They are designed to locate and destroy enemy nuclear weapons before they can be used. The logic of MAD is that you make the use of nuclear weapons unthinkable. The logic of first strike is that you plan for a preemptive first use of nuclear weapons with the expectation that you can destroy the enemy's war-making capabilities. This would theoretically make retaliation impossible.

The national U.S. policy seems to be to prepare to fight and "win" a nuclear war. Political leaders are either stupid enough to believe their own rhetoric about winning a protracted nuclear war or they are planning to develop and use first-strike weapons in a preemptive strike against the Soviet Union. Both options are suicidal, and yet between 1983 and 1989 the U.S.A. will spend $450 billion preparing for nuclear war. More than seventeen thousand new nuclear weapons will be added to the U.S. arsenal throughout the next decade.[76] Many of these weapons, including the MX, Pershing II, and Trident II missiles, are first-strike weapons. They are offensive weapons that target enemy silos. They are powerful and accurate and therefore greatly increase the fear of nuclear war—and thus its likelihood.

The policy of first strike replaces MAD with the illusion of preemptive strikes and winnable first use. Such a policy is itself utterly mad! The Coalition for a New Foreign and Military Policy states the danger:

> For the foreseeable future, neither side has any prospect of getting far enough ahead to matter. The goal of the arms race—first-strike capability—is a will-o'-the-wisp. In practical terms, it simply can never be attained. The futile struggle to attain it is nonetheless dangerous. It is dangerous because each new weapon is a provocation which must be answered for political reasons, and each answer is another provocation.

This action-reaction cycle creates a procurement subculture which is potentially as destabilizing as the weapons themselves. Each side must constantly vilify the other to justify new weapons, until a mentality is created which is like the mentality of nations at war. In a world armed with nuclear missiles, the mentality of war is only a hair's breadth away from war itself. . . .

If we prepare for a first strike against Russia, and they prepare for a first strike against us, war could well become inevitable even though both societies' chance for survival remains zero.[77]

The ultimate cost of the arms race could be global suicide through nuclear holocaust. However, there are other, more immediate consequences. Military spending fuels global inflation because it devours resources and capital for nonproductive growth. It is a poor job-creator per dollar invested and thus robs millions of persons of the opportunity for meaningful employment. It distorts national and international priorities, harnesses the creative energies of researchers and scientists for destructive ends, and robs our children of hope for the future. Most dramatically it victimizes the poor:

• The cost of a single new nuclear submarine equals the annual education budgets of 23 underdeveloped countries with 160 million school-age children.[78]

• Every minute 30 children die for want of food and inexpensive vaccines. During the same 60 seconds the world military budget absorbs $1.3 million of public funds.[79]

• Three-fifths of the population of underdeveloped countries and nearly half of the world population do not have access to safe and adequate drinking water. Each day more than 25,000 persons, most of them children, die for lack of clean drinking water. The World Health Organization estimates that approximately 80 percent of all sickness and disease can be attributed to inadequate water and sanitation. If everyone had safe drinking water and sanitation, infant mortality could be cut by as much as 50 percent. The United Nations estimates that the 10-year cost for meeting the water and sanitation needs of the whole world would be $300 billion, or $30 billion a year.[80] *This 10-year cost is less than the fiscal year 1985 U.S. military budget as requested by the Reagan administration.*

The U.S. poor share a similar fate as their global counterparts. The Children's Defense Fund each year provides a detailed critique of the president's budget in relation to the needs of the poor, particularly children. *A Children's Defense Budget* is obligatory reading for Christians concerned about faith and economic justice.[81] It clearly demonstrates that massive increases in U.S. military spending have come at the expense of the poor:

• One in five American children is poor, one in two black children is poor, and two in five Hispanic children are poor. More than 3.1 million children—3,000 a day—have fallen below the poverty line since 1979. Their 31 percent poverty increase is the sharpest rise in child poverty since statistics have been collected.

• Thirty American children die each day from poverty that could be eliminated by an annual pubic expenditure of $14 billion. Just one-third of President Reagan's proposed military *increase* for 1985 could have lifted every American child out of poverty.

• Each year, 327,000 children are born prematurely in the United States. The president and Congress could not find the $120 million that could provide their mothers with prenatal care. The cost of *one* MX missile is $120 million.

• The food stamp program was cut $7 billion over fiscal years 1982 to 1985. One million recipients were dropped from the program, and an additional twenty million persons had their benefits reduced. School Lunch, School Breakfast, Child Care Food, and Summer Food programs were cut $5 billion (29 percent) over the same period. The $1 million annual subsidy for the four Pentagon executive dining rooms would buy 800,000 school lunches. The corporate dining subsidy ($3.2 billion annually) could buy 2.5 billion school lunches for needy children.

• The president's fiscal year 1985 budget proposed a $41 million cut in foster care and adoption assistance programs. It left untouched the $80 million annual new furniture expenditure for the Defense Department.

• Fewer than 50 percent of U.S. preschool children are immunized against childhood diseases. For example, only 39 percent of black preschool children are immunized against polio. President Reagan proposed a $3 million cut in the childhood immunization program (fiscal year 1982) that would have eliminated immunizations for 75,000 children at risk. Further cuts were proposed in subsequent budgets. *The Defense Department spends $1.4 million each year on shots and other veterinary services for the pets of military personnel.* Additional millions are spent on the transportation of military pets when personnel are transferred. *If veterinary benefits for military pets were eliminated, 35,000 low-income children could be immunized instead.*

SUMMARY

Christians must work to reverse the arms race and disarm the gods of metal. A call to compassionate action can be justified on many grounds. The biblical writers affirm the lordship of Christ over against nation-states. They condemn the use of military power to defend unjust privileges and they insist that shalom (economic and spiritual health) is the foundation on which authentic peace must be built. The biblical writers promote a logic of the majorities based on equity, sufficiency, and the well-being of the poor. The arms race squanders precious resources, victimizes the poor, and threatens to destroy the world God has created. The development of first-strike weapons dramatically increases the likelihood of nuclear war, which could destroy life in a matter of minutes. Christians who are called to be caretakers of creation must resist policies that threaten and even plan for the destruction of the world. Christian peacemakers will likely discover that the path to security passes through a cross. We must resist the idols of nationalism and military power if we are to confront the needless suffering of the poor. Peacemaking will require acts of redemptive suffering.

The following parable, written by John Schuchardt, places the compassionate Samaritan story in the context of the militarism described in this chapter and the necessity for bold and creative action discussed in the final chapter:

Once, in a certain land, there were peasant villages on which napalm bombs fell; mines exploded along the paths and in the fields. Many of the villagers and their children were hurt and many killed.

When it became known that the villagers were suffering, many Christians wondered who was responsible.

A Quaker of good repute thought Congress was responsible and supported efforts to lobby the legislature to cut off funding for such bloodshed. He himself continued to give money to Congress each year on April 15 because the law said it was required.

A Catholic woman, daily communicant, thought upon the slaughter of innocent children and decided to pray each day for peace. She did not think about paying for the bombs and mines, because the money was automatically taken out of her pay each week and sent to the government by her employer.

A Mennonite was troubled in conscience because he knew his taxes were paying for bombs and mines. Thinking about the future, he gave vigorous support to the World Peace Tax Fund which would provide by law that he could elect for reasons of conscience that his taxes be used only for non-military projects. He looked forward in faith to the day when this law would provide solace for his conscience.

A Baptist minister thought that the President was responsible and urged people to vote for a candidate who promised peace. Many in his congregation worked for companies making weapons; others were in the military; all were good, law-abiding citizens. The minister gave thanks to be shepherd of such a fine flock.

An elder in a Hutterite community thought upon the evils of war and recommended a relief effort to care for the families and the injured. He said, "If we knew our taxes were going only for war, of course, we would not pay them. But what can we do? Some of our taxes go for good purposes too, like schools and roads. Besides, our religious life might be disrupted if we were not faithful to the government and obedient to its laws."

Now a young man, an atheist, his eyes and heart open to suffering, made a decision to refuse to pay for war. And when the war against the villages was over and the government increased the military budget by $4 billion and continued to build nuclear weapons, he also refused to pay for this.

Which of these was neighbor to the villagers?[82]

Chapter 6

Hope and Compassionate Action

Yo no puedo callar, no puedo pasar indiferente
ante el dolor de tanta gente. Yo no puedo callar.
No, no puedo callar, me van a perdonar amigos mios,
pero yo tengo un compromiso y tengo que cantar la realidad.

I cannot be quiet, no I cannot pass by indifferently
before the pain of so many persons. I cannot be quiet.
No, I am not able to be quiet, my friends will have to
    forgive me,
but I have a commitment and I have to sing the reality.

                    Chorus to a popular Nicaraguan song
                    by Carlos Mejía Godoy

    We are at a crossroads in human history where Christian faith, hope, and compassion will be severely tested. It is essential that our commitments and our actions reflect both the urgency of the present moment and the long-term nature of social change rooted in faith. Mass hunger, U.S.-supported injustice in Central America, and the threat of nuclear holocaust are fundamentally opposed to our commitments to God, to the poor, and to the survival of creation. A politics of compassion requires that we "sing the reality" through bold personal and collective actions that seek profound social changes. Compassionate actions rarely flow from despair or hopelessness. They are born out of hope. This chapter explores a biblical and practical basis for hope and specific avenues for compassionate action.

    Persons of faith are called on to discern the signs of the times. They are also called to be persons of hope. Unfortunately, honest discernment and true hope often seem at odds. The signs of the times described in previous chapters are disturbing:

- Widespread silence about problems such as hunger and the arms race;
- Acts of compassion blocked, reversed, or distorted by economic and military systems that cause or aggravate hunger;
- Systems of violence, poverty, and repression reinforced by distorted economic priorities, unfair terms of trade, indebtedness, and the use of military power in Central America;
- The arms race expanding its capacity for destruction and its circle of victims.

Equally disturbing, religious faith and theology often support these life-destroying economic and military policies. Many Christians see problems of hunger and armaments as unrelated to faith. Others offer support to repressive but "anticommunist" governments in Central America and elsewhere. Some even go so far as to link God with tyrannical leaders who will protect the American way of life. For example, television evangelist James Robison links "communist propaganda and infiltration" to many of the "satanic forces" that are attacking our land. "Let me tell you something about the character of God," Robison told a group of pastors at a training session on how to mobilize congregations for conservative U.S. political causes. "If necessary, God would raise up a tyrant, a man who might not have the best ethics, to protect the freedom interests of the ethical and the godly."[83] God becomes an advocate of fascism.

Many Christians confuse faith with patriotism. They associate criticism of the nation with criticism of God. U.S. military power is for them an instrument of God's will. Military power becomes an idol in service to nationalistic idols. The religious complicity with nuclear idolatry is nowhere more ironically symbolized than in naming a U.S. trident submarine "Corpus Christi." The body of Christ broken that all might live is now a nuclear submarine capable of destroying the world.

Honest discernment about religious, economic, and military trends provides a formidable challenge to hope. Religion sanctions repression and glorifies false gods. An international economy increases wealth while aggravating poverty, hunger, and inequality. Central Americans groan under the weight of U.S. military and economic policies. At the same time, the global arms race raises the specter of a world coming to a mushrooming, self-inflicted end.

Some choose to ignore problems such as hunger and the arms race because they feel powerless to change things. Even committed organizers must face feelings of disillusionment and despair. I have spent much time working with individuals and groups concerned about problems such as hunger, militarism, and other justice issues. The tension between hope and despair often comes to the surface. I know many committed Christians who refuse to give in to a sense of hopelessness. However, we painfully acknowledge that despite our efforts things sometimes appear to be getting worse rather than better. We give and receive support from each other and ask: "What keeps you going? Where is the hope?"

How can Christians become or remain persons of hope? How can we activate hope in others? Part of the answer lies in stressing the positive signs of the times. Millions of persons, including Christians from the U.S.A. and throughout the world, are working to halt and reverse the arms race. The liberating message of the Bible has encouraged numerous other Christians to become advocates with the poor in opposing social cutbacks and resisting U.S. foreign policies that reinforce repression, hunger, and economic injustice.

In stressing the positive signs of the times it is important to understand that we cannot measure hope by weighing the relative power of two sides of a ledger sheet, one marked "positive signs of the times" and the other "negative." The reality for Christians is that each sign of the times that threatens to breed despair is a call to compassionate action. Each compassionate action is itself a sign of hope that fosters hope in others.

NINE PERSPECTIVES ON HOPE

I am often asked about my ability to remain hopeful and active in the midst of working on difficult problems. I generally respond to such questions with stories about Christians and others I know in Central America who serve and embody hope in the midst of hunger, repression, and the threat of death. I am inspired by their examples and by their pleas that persons like myself work to change U.S. policies that are at the root of so much of the repression they experience. If they are hopeful and compassionate in the midst of incredible danger, then I can embody hope in my life. I also admit that I get discouraged, weary, and frustrated. I try to remember the following practical insights when I find myself drifting away from hope.

First, *it is unrealistic to be hopeful without being open to the pain and suffering of others and to the need for change within my life and within the religious and political institutions of which I am a part.* We must not approach Jesus with questions about "who is my neighbor" or about "eternal life" and then walk away sad because we receive answers such as the need to break our bondage to wealth and relate to our enemies as neighbors. Grace frees Christians to counter despair and embrace compassionate action even when doing so involves painful changes in our lives, values, lifestyles, ideology, and politics.

Secondly, *hope depends on our willingness to honestly confront difficult problems.* My father died of cancer a number of years ago. He started coughing up blood a year or so before he was diagnosed. We were very concerned and greatly relieved when the doctor assured him that, even though coughing up blood was a common sign of lung cancer, in his case it was caused by chronic bronchitis. We eagerly accepted what later proved to be a faulty diagnosis because we were so relieved not to hear the word "cancer." By the time another doctor discovered several tumors, it was too late to help my father.

Coughing up blood was a sign of cancer that we chose to downplay or ignore. The result was costly. In a similar way, there are clear warnings about the dangers of an escalating arms race and its relationship to hunger. If we choose to ignore rather than honestly face these warnings, then we become persons of despair, not hope. Ignorance is not bliss. Ignorance and indifference lead to deadly forms of action or inaction.

I heard Dr. Helen Caldicott speak on the moral, economic, and health reasons for reversing the arms race. She is the author of *Nuclear Madness* and is a founder of Physicians for Social Responsibility, a group of physicians who believe the only cure for health problems associated with nuclear war is prevention. Her critique of the arms race was devastating, well documented, and spoken from the heart. Her willingness to honestly confront the threat of nuclear holocaust gave me hope even though the threat she outlined was depressing. Her understanding and commitment deepened my conviction that the survival of creation is at stake.

Dr. Caldicott tries to shatter what she calls psychic numbness. It is psychic numbness that allows us to deny the depth of a crisis and to live illusionary lives apart from concrete realities such as hunger and the arms race. Caldicott shatters that numbness, raises awareness, and seeks to channel that awareness into determined action. In biblical terms, she is seeking to overcome hardness of heart. She is asking us to be converted to compassionate action in light of present dangers and opportunities.

Thirdly, *hope that is not rooted in specific actions will wither and die.* Hope arises at the moment of honesty when we let ourselves physically and emotionally feel the weight of the obstacles that shackle us. However, hope gives way to despair unless honesty is accompanied by actions that embody hope and give expression to awareness or knowledge. Psychic numbness and hardness of heart are not simply problems of indifference or lack of knowledge. They often arise out of our inability to cope with what we know.

Those who work for social justice often do important illusion-shattering education. However, we often do not adequately help others see avenues for action and reasons for hope. If we help them know more without the hope that is expressed through doing more, then we replace one form of psychic numbness (indifference or ignorance) with another (hopelessness). Specific actions help others express what they know and feel. In addition, it is through action that knowledge is tested and refined. Knowledge without action is like faith without works.

Fourthly, *hope is rooted in friendship and community.* My first response to the question "What can I do?" is to tell persons whatever they do, they should not do it alone. I am very fortunate to have a family that shares and supports my life, commitments, and work. My wife and I have a mutually supportive relationship and we have friends with whom we discuss problems, share hopes and frustrations, recreate, and engage in political action. We get and give support to others at church and we belong to a variety of organizations that help keep us informed and provide us with ample opportunities for creative action (see pp. 123–125, below).

The base Christian communities common in Latin America may be adaptable to our context. There is a strong need for Christians to gather together for mutual support, prayer, Bible study, and action in light of specific community and global needs. The depth of commitment and sharing in the early church (Acts 2:44–46) may need to be resurrected. Personal commitments are vital but hope will be sustained in the struggle for justice only through the collective hope of families and communities that politicize their hope through collective reflection and action.

Fifthly, *if we are to live as a people of hope, then our sense of urgency must be matched by a sense of humor and a spirit of play.* For Christians, play is a manifestation of God's grace. I used to think that anyone who was playful did not know what was going on in the world. I was able to wipe smiles from faces but I was not very effective at communicating or embodying hope. I eventually discovered how important play is to sustaining my own hope and to giving birth to hope in others. There is nothing more depressing and less effective than going out to save the world with sour faces, pained expressions, and suppressed or displaced anger. Such an attitude communicates something other than the substance of one's cause, discourages involvement of new people in social change work, consumes the families of organizers, and disrupts many fine organizations.

We separate ourselves from God's love when we live outside God's spirit. This separation is manifested through apolitical lives that display indifference to human suffering. It is also manifested in the lives of persons committed to reversing the arms race who carry nuclear bombs in their hearts. The results are devastating in either case.

Humor and play are possible when we find the right balance between taking ourselves seriously but not too seriously. Finding this balance requires respect for ourselves and God. We are capable of play when we trust God. In this sense, playfulness has to do with atonement. We are not responsible for saving the world, even though we do participate in salvific works with God. We work to minimize the historical consequences of sin even as we acknowledge that Jesus' death on a cross atones for the sin of the world. This balance between the importance of our action and the primacy of God's action enables us to live responsible and joyful lives. It is possible for us to be playful in the midst of life, in the very heart of struggles for peace and justice.

Sixthly, *hope does not depend on our ability to control all events.* What we do with our lives matters. However, we cannot always be sure that we will accomplish what we set out to do. Compassionate action is possible even in the midst of life situations that are beyond our control. I spent the final three weeks of my father's life at home with him as he died of cancer. I realized fairly quickly that there were limits to what I could do for him. I could be there with him as he was dying. I could comfort, sit in silence, hold his hand, read the Bible, pray, play my dulcimer, adjust his pillow, and share his tears and laughter. I could listen as he shared his feelings, hopes, fears, and spiritual journey, and I could share my own. But I could not control the situation. I could not heal him or take away his pain.

In a similar way, we cannot control all aspects of political life. This is not a plea for inaction or resignation. It is a plea for compassionate action rooted in humility. As an educator and an organizer I try to shape events. For example, I seek to influence U.S. foreign policy in Central America in order to prevent further victimization of the poor. This kind of organizing is essential. However, I accept as a person of faith that things do not always work as smoothly as the plans on a drawing board. Life and politics are complicated, confusing, and at times downright uncontrollable and depressing. Faith frees me for involvement even though there are setbacks and uncertainties.

Seventhly, *we need to act with confidence and anticipation even when things seem depressing.* In pursuit of just social structures we must press on with confidence expecting the fulfillment of God's promises. When the Israelites left Egypt and entered the wilderness they longed to return to slavery (Exod. 14:11–12). I suspect that many of us sometimes long to return to days when faith was a verbal affirmation rather than a journey, and when our political understanding was shaped by myths rather than by the reality of U.S. support for economic injustice and a deadly arms race. The journey of faith that leads to compassionate personal and social action is often difficult but we travel with the assurance that God is with us.

In the New Testament hope is rooted in the crucifixion and resurrection. We are not told that we will win this or that struggle during our lifetime. Rather, we are freed to struggle with a spirit that underscores that we in fact have already won. The hope that is born of the cross and the resurrection is different from optimism. Compassion sometimes requires redemptive suffering. There may be times as we look at U.S. policy in Central America or the global arms race that we will see little reason for optimism. However, there is always the possibility of hope because Christ frees us to be instruments of hope and healing. Politically, our hope is tied to social justice. Spiritually, our hope is rooted in our faithfulness and more importantly in the promise of God's faithfulness to us.

Eighthly, *hope is linked to patience rooted in faith.* Faith and hope encourage not only activism but patience and the ability to wait. Hope requires a persistent, patient, long-term commitment to social justice. We live with the tension between the need for compassionate action to counter immediate injustices and the reality that persons often need time, love, and support in order to change. Faith journeys generally evolve, rather than explode, into commitments to justice. If we patiently nurture these journeys, our patience may be rewarded. If we push ourselves or others too hard or too fast, treasures may be buried beneath an avalanche of misunderstanding, resentment, and fear. Anne Morrow Lindbergh describes how the sea often rewards patience with discoveries of beautiful treasures:

But it must not be sought for or—heaven forbid—dug for. No, no dredging of the sea bottom here. That would defeat one's purpose. The sea does not reward those who are too anxious, too greedy, or too impatient. To dig for treasures shows not only impatience and greed, but lack of faith. Patience, patience, patience, is what the sea teaches. Patience and faith. One should lie empty, open, choiceless as a beach— waiting for a gift from the sea.[84]

The balancing act of the need for immediate action to counter present injustice with the imperative to be patient and nurturing of ourselves and others is also tempered by the awareness that social change will occur over periods of years and even lifetimes. There is no authentic faith or hope without persistence and patience. "No ray of sunshine is ever lost," said Albert Schweitzer. "But the green that it awakes into existence needs time to sprout. All work that is worth anything is done in faith."

Finally, *we must be modest when we discuss the political reasons for hope.* There are no easy solutions to problems of hunger, U.S. policy in Central America, or the arms race. False or inflated promises are costly. In working with others we need to stress specific actions, the importance of their involvement, and the long-term nature of social change. These suggestions together with the affirmation of faith as a journey offer more hope than either silence or inflated claims about what is immediately possible.

When we live without hope, in a very real sense we cease living. It is not only physical death that Jesus overcomes on a cross. It is also the spiritual death associated with hardness of heart and a lack of compassion. Hope, hunger, and the threat of nuclear holocaust demand a compassionate response. They also call us to greater spiritual rootedness, humor, patience, and caring.

AVENUES FOR COMPASSIONATE ACTION

The momentum of the arms race must be broken if present and future generations are to survive. The arms race reduces security to aspects of military power while destroying the essence of shalom. It feeds and is fed by the idols of nationalism and patriotism, which violate the sovereignty of God. It thrives on and encourages an atmosphere of fear and intimidation. It ignores the broader family of God and makes a sham out of the biblical commitment to the poor. It threatens creation, sabotages hope and compassion, and demands ultimate allegiance. It requires Christians to make a decision between gods of metal and the living God who calls us to be peacemakers.

In a similar way, the existence of widespread hunger is intolerable to Christian concern. The suffering of the poor within the present international economy and the repression and hunger in Central America that can be traced to U.S. economic and military policies call Christians to compassionate action. Our faith tells us that God suffers with the poor and that through God's grace we are capable of becoming persons of hope, healing, and compassion.

The previous chapters describe various personal and social obstacles to compassion. The critique of the international economy, U.S. policy in Central America, the arms race, our bondage to ideology and nationalistic idols, and the need to resurrect a liberating faith is a form of *confession* and not just an interesting analysis of religious and social problems. "If we say we have no sin, we deceive ourselves, and the truth is not in us. If we confess our sins, [God] is faithful and just, and will forgive our sins and cleanse us from all unrighteousness" (1 John 1:8–9).

Confession is a necessary step on the road to forgiveness and conversion. When we confess our personal complicity with sinful social structures, we acknowledge the need for personal and social transformation. Confession is followed by repentance, the movement from guilt to heartfelt remorse. Confession and repentance result in forgiveness, which frees us for authentic conversion expressed through compassionate action. "So faith by itself," James 2:17 reminds us, "if it has no works, is dead." The same can be said about knowledge. If we know more about the causes of hunger and the arms race, about a liberating faith, and about the need for personal and social transformation and yet take no action, it means little.

Those who want to respond with compassion to problems such as hunger and the threat of nuclear holocaust should keep four things in mind. First, there are no easy answers, no magical solutions, and no shortcuts to peace and economic justice. Our commitments must be long-term, informed by faith, and nurtured and strengthened with others. Secondly, the problems of hunger and the arms race will not be solved by heroes, heroines, experts, or technicians. Compassion and hope will live or die depending on the action or inaction of ordinary persons. Thirdly, the actions we take must reflect the urgency of the present time. Our actions must be bold, creative, and persistent. Finally, the solutions we seek must reflect our primary commitments to God and to the family of God, while acknowledging special responsibility for working to transform the policies of the United States.

A variety of steps related to individual action and national policy that could lessen the likelihood of nuclear war, reduce the magnitude of world hunger, and help build shalom as a foundation for peace are listed below.

Tax resistance. Tax resistance can take a variety of forms, from earning less than a taxable income to withholding the percentage of federal taxes that pay for war and war preparation. It is a step that many Christians are reluctant to take because of our hesitancy to clash with state authority and because there are often penalties involved.[85] However, it is difficult to reconcile compassion with paying taxes that fuel the nuclear arms race and finance U.S. military policies that protect narrow economic interests at the expense of the poor. Raymond Hunthausen, the Catholic archbishop of Seattle, issued the following plea for tax resistance:

> I would like to share a vision of still another action that could be taken: simply this—a sizeable number of people in the state of Washington, 5,000, 10,000, or half million people refusing to pay 50% of their taxes in nonviolent resistance to nuclear madness and suicide. I think that would be a definite step toward disarmament. Our paralyzed political process

needs that catalyst of nonviolent action based on faith. We have to refuse to give incense—in our day, tax dollars—to our nuclear idol. On April 15th we can vote for unilateral disarmament with our lives. Form 1040 is the place where the Pentagon enters all of our lives, and asks our unthinking cooperation with the idol of nuclear destruction. I think the teaching of Jesus tells us to render to a nuclear-armed Caesar what that Caesar deserves—tax resistance—and to begin to render to God alone that complete trust that we now give, through our tax dollars, to a demonic form of power. Some would call what I am urging "civil disobedience"; I prefer to see it as obedience to God.[86]

Refusal to participate in U.S. military service. There are circumstances that can legitimize Christian participation in national security and military defense. However, it seems impossible to reconcile Christian compassion with military policies that protect a powerful U.S. economic empire at the expense of the poor, and fuel the prospects of nuclear holocaust. It is time for Christians to resign from or refuse induction into the U.S. military establishment. The affirmation that Christ is Lord must take precedence over and offer resistance to the gods of nationalism and militarism.

I had the privilege of traveling in Central America with Peter Fox who upon his return to the U.S.A. announced his resignation from the National Guard. He outlined his reasons for leaving in an article in the *Billings Gazette.* The article reads in part:

I cried for my country in Tegucigalpa, Honduras. I wept for the hurt and the turmoil my country is creating for millions of Latin Americans. . . . I hurt for the hungry, the landless, the children. . . . In Tegucigalpa . . . I saw American soldiers being used as an instrument of foreign policy which says "if it isn't the U.S. model, then it is wrong." I heard U.S. soldiers say they must fight the communist menace in Central America. Many innocents will die before those soldiers . . . find the will-o'-the-wisp they seek. More children will lose their parents and more Salvadorans, Hondurans, Nicaraguans, and Guatemalans will become refugees before the U.S. troops complete their mission.

I see the cruel extension of the arrogance of power, and I see how those in control of my government are abusing the trust given them; and how those abuses translate into death—and holocaust—for innocent peoples. I now see how brute political and economic machinations mean the military I tried to serve so well will be sent out as hired guns. I see how men and women of honest intentions can find themselves wrapped in dishonorable deeds. . . .

For more than 10 years I have served my country as a soldier both on active duty and as a reservist, as a private, sergeant, lieutenant, and captain. . . .

Despite the emotional, patriotic, and financial losses which I will incur,

I cannot continue to serve as an officer in the Army of the United States while it is being used immorally, if not illegally.[87]

Refusal to accept or continue employment in military industries. If we are to resurrect compassion from the clutches of the gods of metal, then we must withhold our labor as a sign of noncompliance with military madness. Many churches have become a hostage to military industries that employ large numbers of their parishioners. The fear of alienating church members and the local community results in a kind of self-censorship of the church. The avoidance of conflict stifles the gospel and imprisons compassion. The world edges away from shalom and closer to nuclear holocaust as Christians build gods of metal following Sunday worship. In Amarillo, Texas, the final assembly point for all U.S. nuclear weapons, Bishop Leroy Matthiesen broke the silence: "We urge individuals involved in the production and stockpiling of nuclear bombs to consider what they are doing, to resign from such activities, and to seek employment in peaceful pursuits."[88]

Christians who ask others to give up military-related employment should also offer emotional and financial support. The church should provide counseling services, help locate alternative employment, find families willing to share income, food, and housing during a period of transition, and participate in national efforts for peace conversion.

Peace conversion. Peace conversion is based on a simple idea: develop and implement plans to convert industries involved in war production to production of useful goods and services, while providing workers with income, training, and benefits during a transition period. One value of peace conversion is that it shifts the burden of the necessary yet disruptive changes of moving to a peaceful economy from workers to society. Military contractors have consistently opposed peace conversion legislation because of high profits and because it would lessen worker dependency.

Withdrawal of investments from military industries and others involved in socially irresponsible production. Individual Christians, churches, and denominations should withdraw investments from military industries and corporations involved in exploitive labor practices, or other activities that aggravate the problem of hunger. Christians must as much as possible break financial complicity with the twin idols of militarism and unbridled capitalism. Alternative uses of funds include increased giving to relief and development agencies, investments in alternative economic enterprises, creation of a "peace pool" to provide financial assistance to workers who resign from military service or industries, and low- or no-interest loans to minority businesses.

Support a nuclear freeze. A nuclear freeze would be a bilateral agreement between the U.S.A. and Soviet Union to halt the production, testing, and deployment of new nuclear weapons systems. The concept of a freeze has been endorsed by numerous religious bodies, including the Catholic bishops of the U.S.A. and the General Convention of the American Lutheran Church.[89] In May 1984, five world leaders from Africa, Asia, Europe, and Latin America called on the United States and the Soviet Union to break the nuclear-negotiations deadlock by halting further production, testing, and deployment of nuclear weapons. The signers of the "four-continent peace initiative" were Indian Prime Minister Indira Gandhi, Mexican President Miguel de la Madrid, Tanzanian President Julius Nyerere, Swedish Prime Minister Olof Palme, and Greek Prime Minister Andreas Papandreou.[90] A nuclear freeze is not an end in itself. It would temporarily halt the arms race at present levels and serve as a starting point for future reductions. The freeze is vital because it would slow the arms race before the advent of first-strike nuclear weapons.

Oppose development of first-strike weapons. We must not fail to grasp the difference between the *dangerous* world of mutual assured destruction (MAD) and the *almost inevitable reality of nuclear holocaust* that would result from the values, logic, and deployment of first-strike weapons. "Trident and other new weapons such as the MX and cruise missiles have such extraordinary accuracy and explosive power," says Archbishop Hunthausen, "that they can only be understood as a buildup to first-strike capability. First-strike weapons are immoral and criminal." The United Methodist Church Board of Global Ministries concurs:

> We also call upon the U.S. government to halt the production and deployment of first-strike nuclear weapons, specifically the MX, Pershing II, and Trident II missile systems. Because these weapons would have the accuracy and explosive power to knock out Soviet missiles while they were still in their underground silos and to destroy Soviet command centers, their deployment could force the Soviets into a launch-on-warning posture. They are thus destabilizing and escalate the danger of nuclear war through accident or misperception.[91]

Ironically, even if the Soviets should develop first-strike weapons (an unlikely prospect if a nuclear freeze were enacted), "parity in first-strike weapons is not a desirable goal and, in fact, . . . with first-strike weapons inferiority is *better* than parity."[92] The fewer first-strike weapons we have, the less likely we are to be destroyed.

Support unilateral steps to break the vicious cycle of escalating weapons expenditures. The U.S. government has always responded to the nuclear stalemate with a commitment to build more sophisticated weapons. The Soviet Union matches the U.S. commitment, and the cycle repeats itself only at more dangerous levels. It is time for bold new action in the opposite direction. The American Lutheran Church at its Eleventh General Convention urged the U.S. government to "show a willingness to take some risks through specific, unilateral steps, inviting adversary nations to reciprocate—understanding that continuation on the present course of nuclear terror carries exceedingly high risks."[93] A good place to start would be for the U.S.A. to stop all first-strike weapon research, production, and deployment, and use the savings to fund UN water and sanitation projects. Only bold actions such as these offer the possibility of moving from suspicion to trust.

Support an international body to oversee a nuclear freeze and mutual reductions in nuclear and conventional weapons. The development of an international agency to verify arms agreements is vital if the arms race is to be reversed. A simple example can illustrate the importance of verification. The Soviet Union has called for a ban on all space weapons. One hundred fifty countries in the UN are on record as opposed to extension of the arms race into outer space (the U.S.A., which has committed billions of dollars to research so-called Star Wars technology, abstained from this vote). The U.S.A. refuses to negotiate a ban, contending that such a ban is not verifiable. The U.S. Congressional Office of Technology Assessment, an agency set up by Congress to give nonpartisan advice to legislators on new scientific and technological projects, insists that such a ban is verifiable.[94] The implication is that the Reagan administration in pursuit of world military supremacy was able to use verification as a smokescreen. If an international agency had the power to verify agreements, destabilizing weapons such as those designed for use in space could be halted before they are produced.

Support and monitor the U.S. Peace Institute. The Catholic bishops' pastoral letter on war and peace recommends the establishment of a national "academy of peace," and urges universities to "develop programs for rigorous interdisciplinary research, education, and training directed toward peaceful expertise."[95] In October 1984 President Reagan signed the U.S. Institute of Peace Act. The purpose of the act is "to establish an independent, nonprofit, national institute to serve the people and the government through the widest possible range of education and training, basic and applied research opportunities, and peace information services as the means to promote international peace, and the resolution of conflicts among the nations and peoples of the world without resort to violence."[96] Concerned Christians should request information about the new institute from their senators, keep themselves informed of its development, make suggestions for research and projects, and register their approval or disapproval of institute initiatives.

Oppose all weapons sales, assistance, and training to repressive governments. U.S. efforts to block or manage social change in Central America and elsewhere are a major cause of hunger. There is no single more important action that Christians could take to help the hungry than to effectively curb U.S. military support for repressive governments that protect unjust economic interests. We should work for strict compliance with laws that restrict economic or military assistance to governments in violation of human rights, including basic economic rights, for close monitoring to ensure that third country suppliers such as Israel are not used to bypass Congress, and for a reorienting of U.S. aid to meet the basic needs of the poorest countries.

Support a new international economic order. The absence of compassion evident in the international economy fosters hunger, poverty, and inequality. It is a major cause of war and social turmoil. In the nuclear age local and regional conflicts that spring from injustice can be the flame that ignites nuclear holocaust. Protecting a way of life based on the exploitation of the poor has always been costly to those who are hungry because of unjust landownership, inappropriate development, and military repression. Today the clinging to such privileges is not only highly immoral but potentially catastrophic. Steps to break the nuclear arms race must be accompanied by efforts to redistribute wealth, power, and global income. Debt relief, higher and more stable commodity prices, and international cooperation to promote production and distribution of goods to meet basic human needs will promote justice and reduce the likelihood of nuclear war.

Legislative action, boycotts, and civil disobedience. It is imperative for Christians to participate in the political process through letter-writing, phone calls, and visits with congressional representatives, participation in political caucuses and forums, and through the ballot box. Christians can also exercise economic power through consumer boycotts and stockholder resolutions.

The urgency of the present situation in Central America and the threat of nuclear holocaust call for these and bolder actions including civil disobedience. Tax resistance, sit-ins, and mass demonstrations against governmental policies and war contractors may be necessary. The movements for the abolition of slavery, women's suffrage, and civil rights would have been slowed or in some cases halted without civil disobedience. For Christians civil disobedience is a matter of faith as well as tactics. The goals of achieving a nuclear freeze, changing U.S. policy in Central America, halting production and deployment of first-strike weapons, and getting the U.S. government to take meaningful unilateral steps to stop the race to oblivion will likely require Christian obedience to God's call to compassion and disobedience to some laws of the state.

Numerous religious groups have participated in a creative form of civil disobedience as a protest against U.S. policy in Central America. Churches and synagogues have declared themselves sanctuaries for Central American refugees denied legal status by the U.S. government. The church action is aimed at preventing the U.S. government from deporting refugees to Central America where they face death or torture. It is also aimed at educating members of the religious and civil community about U.S. policy in Central America.

Involvement in local struggles with the poor. Padre Pedro, when presenting his method of biblical study to the Lutheran churchwomen (see the Introduction), was asked what grace meant to him and how it fit into his theology. "In theory I don't know," he said, "but in my life grace is working with the poor." Working with the poor had changed his life and his faith; it had provided him with new eyes and new ears with which to understand both the biblical message and political reality. Concerns for global justice will be more authentic if they are rooted in communities. Our task at home as well as in Central America is first of all a listening task that can lead to specific actions *with* rather than *for* the poor. Also, fundamental social changes within the U.S.A. are likely to depend on strategic alliances between social classes.

Simpler lifestyles. From 1955 to 1985 the U.S.A. used twice as many minerals and mineral fuels as all humankind throughout prior history.[97] This tremendous squandering of resources to fuel the American way of life contributes to world hunger, accelerates environmental destruction, and leads to

unjust military policies that seek to protect economic privi,
of the poor. A simpler lifestyle is consistent with the bit
majorities, with its stress on equity, sufficiency, and the well-t
It also demonstrates concern for just stewardship and res;
generations. As someone has said, "We do not inherit the earth
from our children." A simpler lifestyle is not a substitute for polit.
a way to pacify guilt. It is one expression of personal values a,   political
commitment. Jørgen Lissner, when he was secretary for Peace and Human
Rights for the Lutheran Federation in Geneva, Switzerland, identified ten ways
in which simpler lifestyles can be meaningful:

- as an *act of faith* performed for the sake of personal integrity and as an
expression of a personal commitment to a more equitable distribution of the
goods of the earth;

- as an *act of self-defense* against the mind-polluting effects of overconsumption;

- as an *act of withdrawal* from the achievement-neurosis of our high-
pressure materialistic societies;

- as an *act of solidarity* with the majority of humankind, those who have no
choice about lifestyle;

- as an *act of sharing* with others what has been given to us, or of returning
what has been stolen by us through unjust social and economic structures;

- as an *act of celebration* of the riches found in creativity, spirituality, and
community with others rather than in mindless materialism;

- as an *act of provocation* (conspicuous underconsumption) to arouse
curiosity leading to dialogue with others about affluence, alienation, poverty,
and social injustice;

- as an *act of anticipation* of the era when the self-confidence and assertive-
ness of the underprivileged force new power relationships and new patterns of
resource allocation upon us;

- as an *act of advocacy* of legislated changes in present patterns of production and consumption in the direction of a new international economic order;

- as an *exercise of purchasing power* to redirect production away from the
satisfaction of artificially created wants toward a supply of goods and services
that meet genuine social needs.[98]

The adoption of simpler lifestyles is not a panacea. It is a meaningful
expression of personal commitment that *frees us from* bondage to material
things and *frees us for* social justice. If adopted on a wide scale, simpler
lifestyles could lead to changes in economic priorities and the availability of
resources to meet the basic needs of present and future generations.

SUMMARY

Our faith and our world are in need of transformation. The voice of God
calling us to repentance, conversion, and compassion can be heard in the voices
of Carmen, Padre Pedro, the Salvadoran and Guatemalan refugees—all those

..Central America who suffer the imperial weight of oppression. The logic of capital is offended by the logic of the majorities, and by the millions of nameless hungry who in fact have names, families, and rights to a future free from hunger, economic oppression, and nuclear madness. Even as we begin to listen, there is the danger that their voices will be muffled amid all the noise of ideology and national symbols. This noise, which can build into a deafening silence, threatens to place us squarely within the biblical paradox of having ears but not hearing.

Faith journeys for both individuals and communities are a process in which the voice of God is discerned in the midst of competing voices. I have argued throughout the pages of this book that our teachers must be the poor. The experience of the poor unlocks the meaning of Scripture; the logic of the majorities judges the validity of economic systems; the well-being of the poor serves as a guidepost for those who seek to embody a politics of compassion in the midst of concrete historical struggles for social justice.

The poor in Central America are calling Christians in the North to repentance and conversion. Their commitment and their suffering are redemptive pleas for compassion. If we heed their call, there may still be time for healing and reconciliation. A regional war in Central America *can* be avoided, hunger *can* be reduced, the arms race *can* be reversed. The acceptance of this call provides hope for the actualization of these possibilities. The refusal of this call guarantees disaster.

Christians in the North via either path—rejection or acceptance of the call—can expect increased suffering. We can remain silent and passively suffer our historical fate with others who remain indifferent to the call to compassion, or we can take risks and act boldly, knowing that no meaningful changes are possible without redemptive suffering. One of the lessons we learn from the poor, and those who choose to stand with them, is that there will always be powerful groups and forces that will seek to crush efforts of the poor for liberation. The fact that by virtue of history or fate we find ourselves living as Christians in the most powerful country in the world speaks to both the importance of our mission and the likely consequences of faithfulness.

The U.S.A. has exported repression throughout Latin America for generations. This repression will come home to roost—it is only a matter of time and a matter of accelerated Christian commitment.

President Reagan submitted to Congress in April 1984 a series of "antiterrorism" laws that throw some light on the danger I am alluding to. One of those laws, labeled "Prohibition against the Training or Support of Terrorist Organizations Act of 1984," is summarized in a press release of April 26 from the White House Office of the Press Secretary:

> This bill would enhance the ability of the Department of Justice to prosecute persons involved in the support of groups and states engaging in terrorism. The bill would prohibit firms or individuals from supporting or cooperating with such groups or states.

The State Department, under this bill, would be given the authority to determine which groups or states are terrorist or offer support for terrorism. For example, the State Department, under the provisions of the bill, could register Nicaragua as a terrorist state and from that day forward any individual or group (for example, solidarity groups) providing ideological or material support to Nicaragua could be tried as terrorists. According to the bill, any determination made by the State Department "shall be conclusive. No question concerning the validity of the issuance of such determination . . . may be raised by a defendant as a defense in or as an objection to any trial or hearing."

This example should be sufficient to illustrate the point that the costs associated with compassion could be high. A politics of compassion will need to be deeply rooted.

I learned a very important lesson from the death of my father. The death that Christians are to fear is not physical death but dying in the midst of life, what the Bible describes as hardness of heart or the death of human compassion. The experience of my father's *physical* death made me acutely aware of the many ways in which I was *spiritually* dying for lack of honesty, commitment, service, faith, hope, and action.

Martin Luther King, Jr., understood the importance of refusing to die in the midst of life:

> If a man happens to be 36 years old, as I happen to be, and some great truth stands before the door of his life, some great opportunity to stand up for that which is right and that which is just, and he refuses to stand up because he wants to live a little longer and he is afraid his home will get bombed, or he is afraid that he will get shot . . . he may go on and live until he is 80, and the cessation of breath in his life is merely the belated announcement of an earlier death of the spirit.[99]

U.S. leadership and participation in structures of injustice results in widespread hunger, political and economic oppression, and an escalating arms race. These problems call Christians to compassionate action involving profound personal and social changes. As Christians living in the U.S.A. we must clearly distance ourselves from nationalistic idols including capitalism and militarism. A liberating theology frees us for service, encourages us to take risks through acts of redemptive suffering and civil disobedience. We are called to be a people of hope in the midst of life, to live honestly, creatively, and compassionately. Christian hope is rooted in the bold assertion that hope can never be extinguished so long as persons of faith resist evil, build justice, and share love.

Notes

1. In Margaret Randall, *Christians in the Nicaraguan Revolution,* Vancouver, New Star Books, 1983, p. 202.

2. In Iben Gjerding and Katherine Kinnamon, eds., *No Longer Strangers: A Resource for Women and Worship,* p. 49 (Lutheran Human Relations, 2703 N. Sherman Blvd., Milwaukee, WI 53210).

3. Taylor Caldwell, *Captains and the Kings,* Garden City, N.Y., Doubleday, 1972, p. 6.

4. Gustavo Gutiérrez, *A Theology of Liberation,* Maryknoll, N.Y., Orbis, 1973, p. 198.

5. Martin Lange and Reinhold Iblacker, eds., *Witnesses of Hope: The Persecution of Christians in Latin America,* Maryknoll, N.Y., Orbis, 1981, pp. 79–80.

6. Ibid., p. 74.

7. Walter Wink, "The Parable of the Compassionate Samaritan," *Review and Expositor* 76 (spring 1979), 199–217. I deeply appreciate Walter Wink's insights into this parable, which serve as a foundation for this chapter.

8. *Christianity and Crisis,* May 1980.

9. "The Salvation Brokers: Conservative Evangelicals in Central America," *NACLA Report,* Jan./Feb. 1984.

10. The Committee of Santa Fe, "A New Inter-American Policy for the Eighties," Washington, D.C., Council for Inter-American Security, 1980, p. 20.

11. *The Holy Bible, Revised Standard Version,* New York and London, Nelson, 1952, p. 70, footnote.

12. Jack A. Nelson, *Hunger for Justice: The Politics of Food and Faith,* Maryknoll, N.Y., Orbis, 1980, p. 58.

13. Ibid., p. 2.

14. Elie Wiesel, *Night,* New York, Hill and Wang, 1958, pp. 70–71.

15. "Messages and Meditations of Mons. Oscar Arnulfo Romero," American Lutheran Church, Task Force on Central America (Our Church and Central America, c/o Office of Church in Society, The American Lutheran Church, 422 S. Fifth St., Minneapolis, MN 55415).

16. "Homilía del Sexto Domingo del Tiempo Ordinario—Las pobrezas de las Bienventuranzas: Fuerza de la verdadera liberación del pueblo," Feb. 17, 1980.

17. *Orientación,* April 13, 1980, based on an interview with José Calderón, a correspondent for the newspaper *Excelsior.*

18. R. Neil Sampson, *Farmland or Wasteland,* Emmaus, Pa., Rodale, 1981.

19. Peter Rosset and John Vandermeer, eds., *The Nicaraguan Reader,* New York, Grove, 1983, p. 302.

20. "Report on the National Bipartisan Commission on Central America," Jan. 1984, p. 43 (hereafter referred to as the Kissinger Commission Report).

21. See Tom Berry et al., *Dollars and Dictators,* Albuquerque, The Resource Center, 1982, pp. 11, 46, 63. Kissinger Commission Report, p. 44.

22. *Central American Report,* vol. 12, no. 7 (May 10, 1982), p. 134.

23. See World Bank, *The Assault on Poverty: Problems of Rural Development, Education, and Health,* Johns Hopkins University Press, 1975, pp. 215–16.

24. See Berry, *Dollars,* p. 23.

25. See Frances More Lappé and Joseph Collins, *World Hunger: Ten Myths,* San Francisco, Institute for Food and Development Policy, 1979, p. 25.

26. Ralph Nader in Robert J. Ledogar, *Hungry for Profits,* New York, IDOC/North America, 1975, p. vii.

27. See Nelson, *Hunger* (n. 12, above), pp. 42–46.

28. See *A Children's Defense Budget: An Analysis of the President's FY 1985 Budget and Children,* Washington, D.C., Children's Defense Fund, 1984, pp. 37, 82.

29. See Jack Nelson-Pallmeyer, "Who Is Totalitarian?: A Comparative Look at Life in Nicaragua and Honduras," *The Other Side,* Feb. 1984, p. 17. See also Philip E. Wheaton, "Inside Honduras: Regional Counterinsurgency Base," Washington, D.C., EPICA Task Force, 1982.

30. In Kurt Greenhalgh and Mark Gruenke, eds., "The Church Martyred: Guatemala," p. 7 (Guatemala Solidarity Committee, P.O. Box 14051, Minneapolis, MN 55414).

31. See *Children's Defense Budget,* p. 18.

32. Berry, *Dollars,* pp. 8–10.

33. Danny Collum, "Trespassing in the Basin," in *Crucible of Hope: A Study Guide for the Churches on Central America,* p. 6 (Sojourners, P.O. Box 29272, Washington, DC 20017).

34. Berry, *Dollars,* pp. 71, 75.

35. Richard Alan White, *The Morass: United States Intervention in Central America,* New York, Harper and Row, 1984, p. 65.

36. Kissinger Commission Report, pp. 96, 102.

37. See Berry, *Dollars,* p. 59.

38. Ibid.

39. "Amnesty Accuses Regime of Many Salvador Deaths," *Minneapolis Tribune,* May 21, 1984.

40. See "Rights Group Urges Duarte to End Abuses," *Washington Post,* Oct. 7, 1984.

41. See Kissinger Commission Report, p. 130.

42. "U.S. Assistance to Guatemala Grows 40%," *Central American Report,* vol. 11, no. 42 (Oct. 26, 1984).

43. In Berry, *Dollars,* p. 13.

44. John Booth, "Toward Explaining Regional Crisis in Central America: Socioeconomic and Political Roots of Rebellion" (unpublished paper).

45. In Berry, *Dollars,* p. 13.

46. In Nelson, *Hunger* (n. 12, above), p. 68.

47. In Berry, *Dollars,* p. 5.

48. "New Inter-American Policy" (n. 10, above), pp. ii, 1, 3.

49. *Minneapolis Tribune,* Sept. 29, 1983.

50. "Behind the Death Squads," p. 20 (continuing from the front cover).

51. See *Crucible of Hope* (n. 33, above), pp. 42–46.

52. See, e.g., Thomas W. Walker, *Nicaragua: The Land of Sandino,* Boulder, Colo., Westview Press, 1981.

53. Many of the statistics I cite on the Nicaraguan economy come from personal meetings with various economists and economic advisors within Nicaragua, including Xabier Gorostiaga of INIES (Instituto de Investigaciones Económicas y Sociales) and

Peter Marchetti, an advisor to the land reform program. Published resources include: "Nicaragua: Give Change a Chance," a publication of the Institute for Food and Development Policy, San Francisco; "Land and Hunger: Nicaragua," Bread for the World (background paper no. 71, Dec. 1983), Washington, D.C.; *An Alternative Policy for Central America and the Caribbean,* published by INIES, Apartado C-16, Managua, Nicaragua.

54. New York, Time Books, 1984.

55. *The Challenge of Peace: God's Promise and Our Response,* Washington, D.C., United States Catholic Conference, 1983, p. 5.

56. Ibid., p. 10.

57. James W. Douglass, *The Non-Violent Cross,* New York, Macmillan, 1969, p. 9.

58. Phillip Berryman, *The Religious Roots of Rebellion: Christians in Central American Revolutions,* Maryknoll, N.Y., Orbis, 1984, p. 312.

59. In Nelson, *Hunger* (n. 12, above), p. 197.

60. Helder Câmara, *The Desert Is Fertile,* Maryknoll, N.Y., Orbis, 1974, pp. 12–13.

61. Maryknoll, N.Y., Orbis, 1981.

62. See Sharon Johnson, "It's 'Bah Humbug' Time for Shoppers Who Run up Heavy Debts over Holidays," *Minneapolis Tribune,* Jan. 24, 1984.

63. See John P. Lewis and Valeriana Kallab, eds., *U.S. Foreign Policy and the Third World: Agenda 1983,* New York, Praeger, 1983. These figures are taken from tables on pp. 210, 212, 214.

64. See "World Arms Expense Heading for $1 Trillion," *Minneapolis Tribune,* May 6, 1984.

65. "Third World Reportedly Spending More for Arms than for Food," Feb. 13, 1984.

66. See Ruth Leger Sivard, *World Military and Social Expenditures 1983,* Washington, D.C., World Priorities, 1983, p. 5.

67. See "U.S.-Soviet Military Facts," *The Defense Monitor,* vol. 11, no. 6 (1982), p. 5.

68. This statement is contained in a fund-raising letter, dated Nov. 23, 1983, from Physicians for Social Responsibility, Cambridge, Mass.

69. See "More Bang, More Bucks: $450 Billion for Nuclear War," *The Defense Monitor,* vol. 12, no. 7 (1983), p. 2.

70. See Nelson, *Hunger* (n. 12, above), p. 81.

71. *Children's Defense Budget* (n. 28, above), pp. 56–59.

72. *Minneapolis Tribune,* Nov. 4, 1983.

73. Ibid.

74. Physicians for Social Responsibility.

75. "President Reagan's Civil Defense Program," *The Defense Monitor,* vol. 11, no. 5 (1982), p. 5.

76. See "More Bang, More Bucks," p. 1.

77. "U.S. and Soviet 'First-Strike' Capabilities," Coalition for a New Foreign and Military Policy, Feb. 1984, p. 5.

78. See Sivard, *Expenditures* (n. 66, above), p. 5.

79. Ibid.

80. See Jack A. Nelson-Pallmeyer, *Water More Precious Than Oil,* Minneapolis, American Lutheran Church, Division for Life and Mission in the Congregation, 1982.

81. *Children's Defense Budget* (n. 28, above); see also the publications for FY 1983 and 1984.

82. In William Durland, *People Pray for Peace,* Colorado Springs, Center Peace Studies, 1982, p. vii.

83. *Bill Moyers' Journal: Campaign Report #3,* 1983, p. 7. This is a transcript of a document aired on WNET, channel 13, by the Educational Broadcasting Corporation.

84. Anne Morrow Lindbergh, *Gift from the Sea,* New York, Random House, 1975, p. 17.

85. See Durland, *People Pray for Peace.*

86. "Military Tax Resistance: A Call to Conversion" (Pax Christi Twin Cities, 1884 Randolph, St. Paul, MN 55105).

87. Peter Fox, "Resignation and Regret," Sept. 25, 1983.

88. *Minneapolis Tribune,* Sept. 19, 1982.

89. *Challenge of Peace* (n. 55, above), p. 60; "Mandate for Peacemaking: A Statement of the American Lutheran Church," p. 8 (adopted Sept. 10, 1982, by the Eleventh General Convention).

90. *Minneapolis Tribune,* May 22, 1984.

91. "The Trident II Missile: It's Time to Stop It," Washington, D.C., Coalition for a New Foreign and Military Policy.

92. " 'First-Strike' Capabilities" (n. 77, above), p. 3.

93. "Mandate for Peacemaking," p. 8.

94. See Tom Wicker, "Reagan's 'Star Wars' Scheme: Nothing More Than a Pipe Dream," *Minneapolis Tribune,* May 21, 1984.

95. *Challenge of Peace,* pp. 70–72.

96. From a brochure, "Santa Cruz Conference for the United States Institute of Peace," May 1985, Santa Cruz Peace Center Committee, Santa Cruz, CA 95063.

97. "A Broken Covenant, A Broken Land," the second of five slideshows in the series *The Land* (Franciscan Communications, 1229 S. Santee St., Los Angeles, CA 90015).

98. Jørgen Lissner, "Ten Reasons for Choosing a Simpler Lifestyle," Geneva, Switzerland, Lutheran World Federation, Study Department.

99. In John and Mary Schramm, *Things That Make for Peace,* Minneapolis, Augsburg, 1976, p. 17.

Organizations and Periodicals

Legislative Networks

Friends Committee on National Legislation, 245 Second St., NE, Washington, DC 20002.
National IMPACT Education Fund, 100 Maryland Ave., NE, Washington, DC 20018; tel. (202) 544-8636. A legislative information network sponsored by the national agencies of twenty-three Protestant, Catholic, and Jewish groups. IMPACT addresses a number of issues including hunger, economic justice, and Central America.
Network, 806 Rhode Island Ave., NE, Washington, DC 20018; tel. (202) 526-4070. A Catholic social justice lobby advocating economic justice for the poor, human rights, decreased U.S. military spending, and an end to the arms race.

World Hunger

Bread for the World, 802 Rhode Island Ave., NE, Washington, DC 20018; tel. (202) 269-0200. A Christian citizens' lobby providing updates on key hunger-related issues and educational information appropriate for discussion and use in churches.
Institute for Food and Development Policy, 1885 Mission St., San Francisco, CA 94103. Provides books and other materials on hunger, including a variety of resources on Central America.
Oxfam America, 115 Broadway, Boston, MA 02116.

Central America

American Friends Service Committee, 1501 Cherry St., Philadelphia, PA 19102; tel. (215) 241-7000. Aid projects and educational materials.
Center for Global Service and Education, Augsburg College, 731 21st Ave. South, Minneapolis, MN 55454; tel. (612) 330-1159. Organizes tours to Mexico and Central America, enabling North Americans to experience firsthand the realities of Latin American life.
Central America Peace Campaign, 318 Fourth St., NE, Washington, DC 20017; tel. (202) 543-0873. A coalition effort to promote alternative U.S. policies for Central America and the Caribbean.
Chicago Religious Task Force on Central America, 407 S. Dearborn St., Room 370, Chicago, IL 60605; tel. (312) 663-4396. National headquarters for the sanctuary movement (Central American refugees in North America).
Committee in Solidarity with the People of El Salvador (CISPES), P.O. Box 50139, Washington, DC 20004; tel. (202) 887-5019.

Friends of the Third World and Cooperative Trading, 611 W. Wayne St., Fort Wayne, IN 46802; tel. (219) 422–6821. National coordinator in the distribution of Nicaraguan coffee and other Nicaraguan products; disseminates related educational materials.

Interreligious Taskforce on El Salvador and Central America, Interchurch Center, 475 Riverside Dr., New York, NY 10115; tel. (212) 870–3383.

National Network in Solidarity with the Guatemalan People, 930 F St., NW, Washington, DC 20004; tel. (202) 483–0050.

National Network in Solidarity with the Nicaraguan People, 2025 I St., NW, Washington, DC 20006; tel. (202) 223–2328.

Policy Alternatives for the Caribbean and Central America (PACCA), c/o The Institute for Policy Studies, 1901 Q St., NW, Washington, DC 20009.

Pueblo-to-People, 5218 Chenevert, #5484, Houston, TX 77004; tel. (713) 523–1197. Distributes Central American handicrafts.

Quixote Center, P.O. Box 5206, Hyattsville, MD 20782. Coordinates the shipping of medical, educational, and other supplies to Nicaragua.

Washington Office on Latin America (WOLA), 110 Maryland Ave., NE, Washington, DC 20002; tel. (202) 544–8045. A church-sponsored ecumenical agency advocating human rights and social justice in Latin America.

Witness for Justice and Peace, c/o SCM, Hart House, University of Toronto, Toronto, Ontario M5S 1A1; tel. (416) 482–1613.

Witness for Peace, National Office, P.O. Box 29241, Washington, DC 20017; tel. (202) 636–3642. Coordinates a nonviolent presence in Nicaragua, and a direct action and public education campaign in the U.S.A.

U.S. Military Policy and the Arms Race

Beyond War, National Office, 222 High St., Palo Alto, CA 94301; tel. (415) 328–7756. A grass-roots response to the threat of nuclear war; prepares and distributes literature, charts, videotapes, etc., for conscientization nationwide.

Center for Defense Information, 600 Maryland Ave., SW, Washington, DC 20004; tel. (202) 484–9490. Publishes *The Defense Monitor,* with extensive data on U.S. and Soviet military capabilities.

The Children's Defense Fund, 122 C St., NW, Washington, DC 20001; tel. (202) 424–9602. Publishes each year *A Children's Defense Budget,* which examines the needs of children and mothers as against the greed of the military establishment.

Clergy and Laity Concerned, 198 Broadway, Room 302, New York, NY 10038; tel. (212) 964–6730. An action-oriented, interfaith, peace and justice organization, with 51 chapters, action groups and affiliates in 28 states; organizes action on economic conversion, racial justice, reversal of the arms race, and justice in Central America.

Coalition for a New Foreign and Military Policy, 120 Maryland Ave., NE, Washington, DC 20002; tel. (202) 546–8400. Represents more than fifty national religious, professional, peace, research, and social action organizations working for a peaceful, noninterventionist, demilitarized U.S. foreign policy.

Council for a Livable World, 11 Beacon St., Boston, MA 02108.

International Physicians for the Prevention of Nuclear War (IPPNW), 225 Longwood Ave., Boston, MA 02115. A federation of national groups dedicated to mobilizing the influence of the medical profession against the threat of nuclear weapons.

Nuclear Weapons Freeze Campaign, National Clearing House, 4144 Lindell Blvd., Suite 404, St. Louis, MO 63108; tel. (314) 533-1169.

Physicians for Social Responsibility, 639 Massachusetts Ave., Cambridge, MA 02139; tel. (617) 491-2754.

Union of Concerned Scientists, 26 Church St., Cambridge, MA 02238.

Tax Resistance

Center on Law and Pacifism, P.O. Box 1584, Colorado Springs, CO 80901; tel. (303) 635-0041.

Pax Christi USA, 3000 N. Mango Ave., Chicago, IL 60634.

Simpler Lifestyles

Alternatives, P.O. Box 429, 5263 Bouldercrest Rd., Ellenwood, GA 30049.

Contributions for Relief and Development

Catholic Relief Services, 1011 First Ave., New York, NY 10022.

Center on Law and Pacifism, P.O. Box 1584, Colorado Springs, CO 80901.

Humanitarian Aid for Nicaraguan Democracy (HAND), 2025 I St., NW, Washington, DC 20006.

Lutheran World Relief, 360 Park Ave. South, 15th Floor, New York, NY 10010.

MAP International, P.O. Box 50, Wheaton, IL 60189-9955. Collects and distributes aid worldwide, especially in response to emergencies.

Periodicals

Envío, a monthly publication of the Instituto Histórico Centroamericano (Managua, Nicaragua); available in English from The Intercultural Center, Georgetown University, Washington, DC 20057.

Multinational Monitor, a monthly publication by Ralph Nader's Corporate Accountability Research Group, 1346 Connecticut Ave., NW, Suite 411, Washington, DC 20036.

NACLA Report, published bimonthly by the North American Congress on Latin America, 151 W. 19th St., New York, NY 10011.

The Other Side, promoting the integration of faith and social action. Jubilee, Inc., 300 W. Apsley St., Philadelphia, PA 19144.

Pax Christi USA, 3000 N. Mango Ave., Chicago, IL 60634.

Seeds Magazine, a publication out of Southern Baptist tradition for Christians concerned about world hunger. Seeds, 222 E. Lake Dr., Decatur, GA 30030.

Sojourners, a magazine for Christians concerned about social justice. Sojourners, P.O. Box 29272, Washington, DC 20017.

Index

Compiled by James Sullivan

Refrain
Praise the Lord, O my soul.

Psalm 146: 4-9

4 Happy are they who have the God of
Jacob for their help! *
whose hope is in the LORD their God;
5 Who made heaven and earth, the seas,
and all that is in them; *
who keeps his promise for ever;
6 Who gives justice to those who are
oppressed, *
and food to those who hunger.

7 The LORD sets the prisoners free;
the LORD opens the eyes of the blind; *
the LORD lifts up those who are
bowed down;
8 The LORD loves the righteous;
the LORD cares for the stranger; *
he sustains the orphan and widow,
but frustrates the way of the wicked.
9 The LORD shall reign for ever, *
your God, O Zion, throughout all
generations.
Hallelujah!

SECOND READING
1 Timothy 6:11-19

AS FOR YOU, man of God, shun all this; aim at righteousness, godliness, faith, love, steadfastness, gentleness. Fight the good fight of the faith; take hold of the eternal life to which you were called when you made the good confession in the presence of many witnesses. In the presence of God who gives life to all things, and of Christ Jesus who in his testimony before Pontius Pilate made the good confession, I charge you to keep the commandment unstained and free from reproach until the appearing of our Lord Jesus Christ; and this will be made manifest at the proper time by the blessed and only Sovereign, the King of kings and Lord of lords, who alone has immortality and dwells in unapproachable light, whom no man has ever seen or can see. To him be honor and eternal dominion. Amen. As for the rich in this world, charge them not to be haughty, nor to set their hopes on uncertain riches but on God who richly furnishes us with everything to enjoy. They are to do good, to be rich in good deeds, liberal and generous, thus laying up for themselves a good foundation for the future, so that they may take hold of the life which is life indeed.

GOSPEL
Luke 16:19-31

JESUS SAID, "There was a rich man, who was clothed in purple and fine linen and who feasted sumptuously every day. And at his gate lay a poor man named Lazarus, full of sores, who desired to be fed with what fell from the rich man's table; moreover the dogs came and licked his sores. The poor man died and was carried by the angels to Abraham's bosom. The rich man also died and was buried; and in Hades, being in torment, he lifted up his eyes, and saw Abraham far off and Lazarus in his bosom. And he called out, 'Father Abraham, have mercy upon me, and send Lazarus to dip the end of his finger in water and cool my tongue; for I am in anguish in this flame.' But Abraham said, 'Son, remember that you in your lifetime received your good things, and Lazarus in like manner evil things; but now he is comforted here, and you are in anguish. And besides all this, between us and you a great chasm has been fixed, in order that those who would pass from here to you may not be able, and none may cross from there to us.' And he said, 'Then I beg you, father, to send him to my father's house, for I have five brothers, so that he may warn them, lest they also come into this place of torment.' But Abraham said, 'They have Moses and the prophets; let them hear them.' And he said, 'No, father Abraham; but if some one goes to them from the dead, they will repent.' He said to him, 'If they do not hear Moses and the prophets, neither will they be convinced if some one should rise from the dead.' "

Twentieth Sunday after Pentecost   **Proper 21**

COLLECT

Traditional

O GOD, who declarest thy almighty power chiefly in showing mercy and pity: Mercifully grant unto us such a measure of thy grace, that we, running to obtain thy promises, may be made partakers of thy heavenly treasure; through Jesus Christ our Lord, who liveth and reigneth with thee and the Holy Spirit, one God, for ever and ever. *Amen.*

Contemporary

O GOD, you declare your almighty power chiefly in showing mercy and pity: Grant us the fullness of your grace, that we, running to obtain your promises, may become partakers of your heavenly treasure; through Jesus Christ our Lord, who lives and reigns with you and the Holy Spirit, one God, for ever and ever. *Amen.*

FIRST READING
Amos 6:1-7

THUS SAYS THE LORD: "Woe to those who are at ease in Zion, and to those who feel secure on the mountain of Samaria, the notable men of the first of the nations, to whom the house of Israel come! Pass over to Calneh, and see; and thence go to Hamath the great; then go down to Gath of the Philistines. Are they better than these kingdoms? Or is their territory greater than your territory, O you who put far away the evil day, and bring near the seat of violence? Woe to those who lie upon beds of ivory, and stretch themselves upon their couches, and eat lambs from the flock, and calves from the midst of the stall; who sing idle songs to the sound of the harp, and like David invent for themselves instruments of music; who drink wine in bowls, and anoint themselves with the finest oils, but are not grieved over the ruin of Joseph! Therefore they shall now be the first of those to go into exile, and the revelry of those who stretch themselves shall pass away."

Other Orbis Titles . . .

BROKEN BREAD, BROKEN BODIES
The Eucharist and World Hunger
by Joseph A. Grassi
Although the Lord's Supper bears symbolic and sacramental meaning, it is, at a more fundamental level, simply a sharing of food. Joseph Grassi shows how a meaningful celebration of the Eucharist can mobilize effective individual and community action to end world hunger. This is a popular book that should be in every parish library.
   The author is Professor of Religious Studies at the University of Santa Clara, California.
no. 193-4   128pp. pbk. $6.95

WORLD HUNGER
The Responsibility of Christian Education
by Suzanne Toton
"I believe this is the one best book available for serious analysis and action on world hunger. It brings together effectively the dimensions of the problem that must be considered as a whole: emergency food relief, aid and trade, multinational structures, and analysis of "root causes" as well as practical suggestions for study and action."
William B. Kennedy,
Union Theological Seminary
   Suzanne Toton is assistant professor of Christian Living and Religious Education in the Religious Studies Department, Villanova University.
no. 716-9   224pp. pbk. $7.95

HUNGER FOR JUSTICE
The Politics of Food and Faith
by Jack A. Nelson
An analysis of the ways in which the biblical teachings on poverty and hunger can lead to a greater understanding of this problem as it exists today.
   ". . . a comprehensive look at the colonial roots of poverty and underdevelopment in the Third World and at the ways in which U.S. economic and military policies reinforce existing inequalities. All the major issues in the debate over world hunger—the role of multinational corporations, the crisis in American values, overpopulation, the Green Revolution—are treated, at a level the newly interested reader can appreciate."
Library Journal
no. 196-9   230pp. pbk. $7.95

REVOLUTIONARY PATIENCE
by Dorothee Sölle

A collection of 26 fervent poems that attempt to make sense, in light of the gospel, of a world brutally scarred by oppression.

"... full of precise emotions, powerfully evoked. And full of challenges to human complacency."   *Sojourners*

German theologian Dorothee Sölle divides her time between New York City, where she teaches as Union Theological Seminary, and Hamburg.

no. 439-9   82pp. pbk. $5.95

SOCIAL ANALYSIS
Linking Faith and Justice
by Joe Holland and Peter Henriot

This study describes the task of social analysis and its relevance to social justice action. According to Joe Holland and Peter Henriot, the way people see a problem determines how they will respond to it. Social analysis is a result of "seeing a wider picture" of the problem—exploring structural issues, examining causal linkages, identifying key factors, and tracing long term trends. This approach, they assert, will initiate action capable of affecting profound social change. The book provides illustrations of analytical approaches to various problems and explores the suggestions and questions they raise for pastoral response.

"... a provocative essay that is particularly valuable in highlighting the role of the social sciences in effective applications of faith values."   *Sociological Analysis*

Peter Henriot and Joe Holland are director and staff member, respectively, of the Center of Concern, Washington, D.C.

no. 462-3   118pp. pbk. $6.95

THIRD WORLD RESOURCE DIRECTORY
A Guide to Organizations and Publications
edited by Thomas Fenton & Mary Heffron

A comprehensive guide which lists and describes hundreds of resources for educators, committed church and political activists, and other concerned citizens interested in Third World issues. The directory is divided into two parts: by area and by issues. The areas include Third World, Africa, Asia and the Pacific, Latin America and the Caribbean, and the Middle East. The issues addressed are Food, Hunger, Agri-business, Human Rights, Militarism, Peace, Disarmament, Transnational Corporations, and Women. Resources include organizations, books, periodicals, pamphlets and articles, films, slide shows, videotapes, and simulation games. Comprehensively cross referenced and indexed.

"... there is no other source that provides such a wealth of information."   *Choice*

no. 509-3   304pp. pbk. $17.95

OF WAR AND LOVE
by Dorothee Sölle

In this moving and beautifully written volume of poetry and prose, Dorothee Sölle cries out against war and violence citing a number of situations and attitudes she sees as fostering them—the arms race, oppression in Latin America, racism, and sexism. She asks Christians to voice their oppositions to war and its underlying causes and to respond through a measure of nonviolent resistence.

"*Of War and Love* is a book like a banner, a book like a broadsheet. Dorothee Sölle is that rare human: a theologian who is not afraid to be loud and faithful and lucid about unmentionable topics." *Daniel Berrigan, S.J.*

no. 350-3 **172pp. pbk.** **$7.95**

PARENTING FOR PEACE AND JUSTICE
by Kathleen and James McGinnis

How do parents act for justice without sacrificing their own children? How do they build family community without isolating themselves from the world? In this practical and insightful volume, Kathleen and James McGinnis address these and many other problems families may encounter in their effort to integrate social and family ministry. Topics discussed include stewardship, nonviolence both in and outside the family, promoting sexual equality in the family, multiculturalizing family life, and inviting children to participate in social action.

"The guide is filled with exercises, readings, and worksheets to supplement the reading of the book and makes its contents all the more real in our lives. This combination is indispensable for educators and families alike." *Religious Education*

Kathleen and James McGinnis are staff members of the Institute for Peace and Justice in St. Louis and the parents of three children.

no. 376-1 **143pp. pbk.** **$6.95**

WAR OR PEACE?
The Search for New Answers
edited by Thomas A. Shannon

A collection of 13 essays that address the issues of both pacifism and just-war theory with respect to ethical theory, political strategy, and the responsibility of individuals and the community.

". . . an invaluable aid to understanding this most serious problem." *America*

"Shannon's book will be a strong resource to introduce students to the issues without theological pretentiousness or denominational provincialism." *Mission Focus*

no. 750-9 **256pp. pbk.** **$9.95**

WORLD CITIZEN
Action for Global Justice
by Adam Daniel Corson-Finnerty

The author's aims in writing this book were to further educate readers on a variety of global issues and to encourage them to work toward solving some of the problems that exist by becoming actively involved in groups formed for that purpose. The issues discussed include economic justice, world resource consumption, pollution, nuclear armaments, and discrimination. Part two of the book gives brief descriptions (including addresses) of a wide variety of organizations involved with these issues and also provides a list of additional reading materials.

"Corson-Finnerty explains complex issues in language easily understood by the average layperson. An unusually good general introduction and sound book on global issues." *Library Journal*

Adam Corson-Finnerty currently works as Administrator in the International Division of the American Friends Service Committee. He is also actively involved with an action group called *American Christians for the Abolition of Torture.*

no. 715-0   **178pp. pbk.**   **$6.95**

NO MORE PLASTIC JESUS
Global Justice and Christian Lifestyle
by Adam Daniel Corson-Finnerty

According to Adam Corson-Finnerty, overconsumption of the world's resources by affluent First World countries is the major cause of poverty and underdevelopment in Third World nations. In *No More Plastic Jesus* he asserts that global consumption patterns can be restructured so that all the world's people can attain a just standard of living. To attain this goal he advocates and explains a number of strategies including proper planning and distribution of resources, maintaining ecological soundness, sharing personal wealth with the poor, and commitment to a less wasteful lifestyle. He makes a special plea to the churches to join this effort by promoting global justice both through their teachings and their example.

"A great book for adult study and conscience formation." *Religion Teachers Journal*

no. 341-4   **223pp. pbk.**   **$6.95**